AF680257

The Investor's IPO

Navigating Risk and Opportunity in the Global IPO Market

The Investor's IPO

Navigating Risk and Opportunity in the Global IPO Market

Peter Goldstein

EXCHANGE LISTING
PUBLISHING

The Investor's IPO
Navigating Risk and Opportunity in the Global IPO Market
© 2025 by Peter Goldstein

All rights reserved solely by the author. The author guarantees all contents are original and do not infringe upon the legal rights of any other person or work. This book or parts thereof may not be reproduced in any form, stored in any retrieval system, or transmitted in any form by any means—electronic, mechanical, photocopy, recording, or otherwise—without prior written permission of the publisher, except as provided by United States of America copyright law.

ISBN-13:
979-8-9891711-3-2 Paperback
979-8-9891711-4-9 Hardcover
979-8-9891711-5-6 eBook
LCCN: 2025909646

Exchange Listing Publishing
Fort Lauderdale, Florida

www.exchangelistingllc.com

Contents

FOREWORD

Over nearly 40 years on the New York Stock Exchange floor, I have seen every cycle, from bubbles to busts, and watched thousands of companies ring the bell and take their shot at the public markets. But one thing remains constant: the public markets are about belief in a business, in a founder and in a company's ability to grow, scale and deliver over time.

If you're a retail investor trying to get in on that story from the very beginning, you need more than headlines. That's why this book matters.

Peter Goldstein is a founder, operator and a battle tested small and micro-cap capital markets advisor. He has guided emerging growth companies through the IPO journey in every forum, from the boardroom to the roadshow to the bell, and he knows who gets access and why so many get left out.

In The Investor's IPO he pulls back the curtain with no spin or sales pitch. You get a clear map for retail investors who want to take part in the next wave of public companies and do it right. He decodes everything from pricing mechanics and allocations to prospectus details and alternative listing routes such as SPACs, Reg A plus, direct listings and global exchanges.

What I appreciate most is that this book isn't just about mechanics but about the mindset. Peter knows the emotional ride of investing, the fear, the FOMO and the second guessing. He equips you with tools to stay grounded, smart and strategic so you can decide whether a deal makes sense.

I have had a front row seat to some of the most iconic IPOs in market history, Alibaba and LinkedIn among them. I still remember the roar when Alibaba debuted, a moment that proves preparation, clarity and trust make all the difference.

And that trust is at the heart of my relationship with Peter. Through bull runs and bear markets, successes and setbacks, we've grown together—our mutual respect and confidence deepening with each cycle, emerging stronger on the other side.

If you are ready to truly understand how the public markets work and to participate with confidence, this is a must read. The edge belongs to those who do the work, and Peter Goldstein has done the work. Now you can too.

See you at the bell.

Peter Tuchman
Wall Street Icon

ACKNOWLEDGMENTS

This book is the culmination of not just research and writing, but a lifetime of experience, relationships, and resilience. I'm deeply grateful to those who have stood beside me, not only in bringing this project to life, but throughout the entrepreneurial journey that shaped it.

To Eva. Thank you for your unwavering support, especially during the long, focused hours this book required. Your presence, trust, and partnership carried me through more than you know.

To my writing partner, Shirley. Your insight, patience, and support helped bring clarity to the page and structure to the message. I couldn't have done this without you.

To my family and loved ones. Your steady support and love are my foundation.

To my team at Exchange Listing and Emmis Capital. Thank you for believing in this mission and showing up with heart and commitment.

To the mentors, partners, clients, colleagues, and the entrepreneurs and leaders I have had the privilege to serve. Your trust and challenges helped me grow. You are the reason this book exists.

To the interns who supported the research and contributed meaningfully to this project. Your curiosity, effort, and fresh perspective were felt throughout. I wish you the very best and hope this experience becomes a meaningful part of your journey ahead.

With deep gratitude and respect,
Peter

INTRODUCTION

Opening the Door to a New Era of IPO Investing

In the ever-evolving world of finance, few opportunities inspire excitement and uncertainty like an Initial Public Offering (IPO). Whether you're a seasoned investor or new to capital markets, the prospect of participating in a company's public debut holds the allure of growth, transformation, and strategic foresight. Yet, beneath the headlines and bell-ringing ceremonies lies a complex, often opaque landscape where access, information, and timing define outcomes. This book is your guide through that landscape.

The Investor's IPO was written to demystify the IPO process and empower a broader community of investors to participate with clarity and confidence. While IPOs have traditionally been the domain of institutional investors and high-net-worth individuals, the democratization of markets, driven by technology, regulatory reform, and retail investor momentum, is rapidly changing the rules of the game. Today, more investors than ever are seeking to understand not just how to access IPOs but also how to evaluate them with the same rigor and discipline as the professionals.

Over the past decade, the IPO market has witnessed profound shifts. New listing mechanisms such as SPACs and direct listings have challenged the traditional model. Digital platforms have opened retail access. In addition, sectors like technology, life sciences, and AI have reshaped investor expectations around growth, risk, and innovation. This book explores those shifts in detail and equips readers with the tools to navigate an increasingly dynamic and inclusive IPO ecosystem.

What sets this book apart is its structured, practical approach. Across twelve chapters, you'll find clear explanations, expert insights, and actionable strategies to decode the IPO journey. These range from the historical evolution and economic significance of public offerings to evaluating financial fundamentals, understanding the IPO prospectus, managing risks, and anticipating future trends. Each chapter is enriched with real-world case studies, summaries, and investor takeaways, to guide you as you learn.

Importantly, this book doesn't just focus on institutional strategies. It centers on the modern investor: an individual navigating a sea of information and seeking a signal amidst noise. Whether you're investing in a high-growth startup going public or evaluating foreign IPOs on U.S. exchanges, *The Investor's IPO* provides the playbook to make informed, responsible decisions.

Behind these pages are decades of experience. Author Peter Goldstein, a serial entrepreneur and IPO advisor, brings insights forged through years in the trenches of the capital markets. With close to forty years of international business experience, Peter combines practitioner expertise with an investor's mindset. This follow-up to his bestselling book, *The Entrepreneur's IPO*, marks the next step in his mission to bridge the knowledge gap and foster smarter participation in public markets.

As the global IPO landscape continues to evolve, one thing remains clear: success in IPO investing is not reserved for the few. It belongs to those who understand the process, assess the risks, ask the right questions, and position themselves with foresight. With the right guidance, that investor can be you.

Whether you're looking to refine your IPO strategy, better understand market dynamics, or simply explore new opportunities, this book is your companion. Let's open the door and step into the next era of IPO investing.

CHAPTER 1

Modern IPO Essentials

UNDERSTANDING TODAY'S MARKET AND THE ORIGINS OF IPO INVESTING

DEFINING AN IPO

An Initial Public Offering (IPO) marks the pivotal transition of a company from private to public ownership. In this process, a company offers its shares to the public for the first time on a stock exchange, primarily to raise capital for expansion, innovation, or strategic initiatives. But an IPO is far more than a capital-raising event; it's a transformational milestone that introduces new responsibilities, opportunities, and risks.

For investors, an IPO represents a rare inflection point: the opportunity to invest in a company as it enters public markets, often before its valuation fully reflects its long-term potential. IPOs can provide access to early-stage exposure in high-growth sectors, including emerging technologies, healthcare innovation, and sustainable infrastructure. However, they also require careful analysis, as the data available is typically limited to the company's pre-IPO filings and roadshow materials.

From a structural standpoint, going public brings heightened regulatory scrutiny, mandatory financial disclosures, and the need for disciplined corporate governance. Companies must now meet the expectations of a broader and more diverse shareholder base, including institutional and retail investors, and align operations with public market standards.

For founders and early backers, an IPO often provides a liquidity event, allowing partial or full realization of returns. For the company, it can open access to deeper capital markets, improve brand visibility, and attract top-tier talent through equity compensation programs.

In essence, an IPO is both a financial mechanism and a strategic signal. It reflects a company's readiness to scale, its confidence in long-term viability, and its willingness to operate under the scrutiny and discipline of the public markets. For investors, understanding the IPO process is foundational to evaluating risk, opportunity, and alignment with their broader portfolio strategy.

THE EVOLUTION OF IPOS IN CONTEMPORARY MARKET DYNAMICS

Historically, IPOs were largely reserved for established, blue-chip corporations, transactions shaped and led by major investment banks, with limited access for smaller firms and retail investors. The underwriting process was opaque, capital-intensive, and often geared toward institutional networks. But over the past two decades, that landscape has shifted dramatically.

Small and micro-cap companies, once peripheral players in the public markets, have become increasingly visible, in part due to regulatory reforms such as the Jumpstart Our Business Startups (JOBS) Act of 2012. The JOBS Act also introduced provisions such as "testing-the-waters" communications, which allowed emerging growth companies to gauge investor interest before filing publicly. These changes reduced the cost and complexity of going public and, in doing so, diversified the IPO pipeline across sectors and market caps.

At the same time, advances in digital infrastructure have modernized the IPO process. Online investor platforms, digital roadshows, and algorithm-driven book-building tools have made it more efficient, data-rich, and scalable. As a result, companies in sectors like technology, biotechnology, and clean energy, many of which are asset-light but innovation-heavy, have embraced the public markets earlier in their life cycle.

For investors, this evolution expands access and opportunity. Today's IPOs are not confined to mega-cap industrials; they include SaaS platforms, AI disruptors, precision medicine firms, and fintech challengers. These companies may offer outsized growth potential but also introduce new kinds of risk: shorter operating histories, more volatility, and higher sensitivity to market sentiment. Understanding the forces shaping these newer entrants is critical to evaluating long-term value versus hype.

The emergence of alternative listing methods, most notably direct listings and Special Purpose Acquisition Companies (SPACs), further underscores the changing dynamics. Each model brings distinct implications for valuation transparency, investor protection, and post-listing performance.

Ultimately, IPOs have evolved from rigid, one-size-fits-all processes into strategic instruments tailored to a company's capital needs, market positioning, and growth narrative. For investors, this evolution calls for a more nuanced lens, one that considers not just what a company does but how and why it's choosing to go public now.

THE HISTORICAL ROOTS OF IPO INVESTING

To understand the modern IPO and why it continues to be a vital mechanism for companies and investors, it's essential to trace its historical roots. The first known IPO took place in 1602, when the Dutch East India Company issued shares to the public to fund its overseas trade operations. The Dutch East India Company (VOC) not only issued shares but also introduced features like limited liability and secondary trading on an exchange, practices that laid the foundation for modern stock markets. In doing so, it created a new economic model: distributed ownership through equity capital. This early innovation not only financed one of the most powerful trading empires of the era but also laid the groundwork for what we now recognize as the modern stock exchange.

The concept of publicly owned capital spread gradually, gaining momentum in the eighteenth and nineteenth centuries. However, the path was not without turbulence. The South Sea Bubble of 1720 is one of the earliest and most consequential examples of unchecked speculation fueled by misinformation. Investors, seduced by inflated promises and lacking access to reliable data, poured capital into the South Sea Company, only to watch it collapse spectacularly. The fallout was devastating, triggering widespread financial ruin and shaking public trust in capital markets.

From an investor's perspective, the South Sea Bubble highlighted enduring risks: overvaluation, hype-driven demand, and inadequate regulatory oversight. In response, the British government passed the Bubble Act, one of the first attempts to regulate joint-stock companies. Though imperfect, it marked an early recognition that investor protection and market integrity were essential to the sustainability of public markets.

By the early twentieth century, IPOs were commonplace, but safeguards were still minimal. Then came the

1929 stock market crash, a watershed moment in financial history. The ensuing Great Depression laid bare the consequences of rampant speculation, weak corporate disclosure, and uneven investor access to information. The damage to market value and public trust was unprecedented.

In response, the United States enacted two foundational laws: the Securities Act of 1933 and the Securities Exchange Act of 1934. Together, they created the regulatory architecture still in place today. These laws introduced mandatory disclosures for public offerings, established civil liability for misstatements, and created the Securities and Exchange Commission (SEC) to oversee and enforce compliance.

For investors, these reforms fundamentally changed the nature of IPO investing. They shifted the playing field from speculative guesswork to research-driven evaluation, elevating transparency and corporate accountability as cornerstones of the public markets. The IPO was no longer just a fundraising event; it became a regulated gateway to broad-based shareholder participation.

CASE STUDY: THE DUTCH EAST INDIA COMPANY - THE BIRTH OF PUBLIC CAPITAL MARKETS

In 1602, the Dutch East India Company (Vereenigde Oostindische Compagnie, or VOC) made history by launching what is widely recognized as the world's first initial public offering (IPO). Based in Amsterdam, the VOC invited the public to invest in its trade expeditions to Asia, introducing the revolutionary concept of distributed ownership through equity capital. For the first time, ordinary citizens, not just royals or aristocrats, could purchase shares in a private enterprise and share in its profits and risks.

This innovation marked the genesis of the modern capital markets. The VOC's IPO raised substantial capital, enabling it to establish a dominant global trading network that would reshape the balance of economic power in the seventeenth century. Crucially, investors were granted limited liability, protecting them from losses beyond their initial investment. The shares issued were tradable on a newly emerging secondary market. This development would later evolve into the Amsterdam Stock Exchange, arguably the world's first formal securities market.

The significance of the VOC's IPO cannot be overstated. It demonstrated how pooled capital could fund ambitious, high-risk ventures that would otherwise be out of reach. It also revealed the importance of investor protections, transparency, and governance. These principles remain foundational to today's IPO landscape. In many ways, the VOC was not just a trading company. It was a prototype of the modern public corporation.

The legacy of the VOC endures. Its IPO laid the groundwork for corporate finance as we know it, influencing financial systems for centuries. For modern investors, the story of the VOC serves as a powerful reminder. Public capital can scale ideas beyond borders, but long-term success depends on trust, transparency, and a clear alignment between investor interests and business ambition.

THE DOT-COM BUBBLE: LESSONS IN HYPE AND FUNDAMENTALS

The late 1990s and early 2000s marked one of the most frenzied periods in IPO history, a speculative boom fueled by the rapid rise of internet-based companies. Investor enthusiasm reached fever pitch as traditional valuation metrics were cast aside in favor of user growth, domain names, and market potential. Some companies during the dot-com bubble had viable business models but were overvalued due to speculative investor behavior. For example, while firms like Pets.com failed quickly, others like Amazon survived and thrived by adapting their models post-bubble.

For investors, the dot-com era was exhilarating and deeply instructive. On the one hand, it demonstrated how capital markets could accelerate innovation and industry transformation. On the other hand, it revealed the dangers of exuberance untethered from fundamentals.

While outliers like Amazon and eBay ultimately fulfilled their growth narratives and became generational success stories, many others, such as Pets.com, Webvan, and Boo.com, flamed out quickly, unable to monetize user acquisition or control operational burn rates. These companies raised hundreds of millions in IPO proceeds, only to fail within months of listing.

From an investor's perspective, the core lesson of the dot-com bubble is timeless: sustainable growth matters more than hype. Strong financial discipline, a viable business model, and clear unit economics are not optional; they are prerequisites for long-term success in public markets.

The era also served as a case study in how speculative manias form. Easy access to capital, aggressive media coverage, and the rise of retail investing created a feedback loop that inflated valuations far beyond intrinsic value. Investor psychology played a central role, anchored by fear of missing out (FOMO), herding behavior, and narrative bias.

In the aftermath of the bubble's burst, trillions in market value were wiped out, and investor confidence took years to recover. However, the regulatory and institutional responses helped shape today's more disciplined approach to IPO vetting and valuation. Venture capital firms, underwriters, and institutional investors became more rigorous in assessing fundamentals, and the public markets began to place renewed emphasis on profitability, path-to-scale, and capital efficiency.

For modern investors, the dot-com bubble remains a critical reference point. It underscores the importance of questioning prevailing narratives, performing independent analysis, and understanding the macro context that drives IPO valuations. It also offers a reminder that innovation and speculation often arrive hand in hand, but only companies with durable models and operational discipline endure.

MODERN IPO PROCESS: INCLUSIVITY AND INNOVATION

The IPO process has undergone a profound transformation in the past decade. Once exclusive and opaque, dominated by private roadshows and institutional allocations, today's IPO landscape is increasingly inclusive, data-driven, and responsive to market dynamics and investor demand.

Historically, the IPO path favored large investment banks and their institutional clients. Pricing decisions, share allocations, and access were tightly controlled, often leaving retail investors with limited entry points and little transparency. But the regulatory reforms introduced by the JOBS Act of 2012 changed that equation. Emerging growth companies gained the ability to confidentially file their IPO paperwork, reducing early reputational risk and creating more flexibility in timing. This shift lowered barriers to entry and encouraged a broader swath of companies to consider going public.

Concurrently, technology has opened new channels for investor access. Online brokerage platforms and mobile-first investing apps now offer IPO allocations to individual investors, an opportunity that was once the exclusive domain of institutional funds. These platforms have also democratized the flow of information, providing real-time access to prospectuses, investor presentations, and market sentiment data.

Virtual roadshows, increasingly standard since the COVID-19 pandemic, have further disrupted traditional dynamics. By replacing in-person meetings with digital presentations, companies can now reach a broader audience of investors in less time and at a lower cost. This not only levels the playing field but also allows for more consistent messaging, faster feedback loops, and broader geographic reach.

Perhaps the most visible innovations in IPO structure have come from alternative listing mechanisms. Direct listings allow companies to enter the public markets without issuing new shares or relying on underwriters to set pricing. This approach appeals to firms with strong brand recognition and ample private capital, offering market-based price discovery and reducing dilution. On the other hand, Special Purpose Acquisition Companies (SPACs) flip the traditional IPO timeline by raising capital first and identifying a target company later. For certain companies, particularly those with complex business models or time-sensitive growth needs, SPACs offer speed, flexibility, and negotiation leverage.

For investors, these developments require a deeper understanding of structure and intent. The path a company chooses to go public can reveal a great deal about its strategy, capital needs, and governance readiness. Direct listings may suggest operational maturity and brand equity; SPACs may indicate a willingness to trade speed for scrutiny. And retail access to IPOs introduces opportunity and risk, particularly when investor demand outpaces rigorous due diligence.

Ultimately, the modern IPO process is no longer a one-size-fits-all proposition. It is a toolkit of pathways, shaped by technology, regulation, and market innovation. For investors, navigating this terrain requires more than just access; it demands analysis, context, and a sharp eye for alignment between structure, story, and substance.

CASE STUDY: GOOGLE - REDEFINING THE IPO PLAYBOOK

In 2004, Google disrupted IPO norms with its Dutch auction approach; however, this method did not entirely bypass traditional underwriters. Google still engaged major investment banks like Morgan Stanley and Credit Suisse to assist with its offering. The Dutch auction was intended to democratize share allocation but faced criticism for being complex and not achieving significant price stability on day one. Shares were priced at $85, opened at $100.01, and closed at $100.34 on day one. The IPO raised $1.67 billion, valuing the company at $23 billion.

Initially met with skepticism, Google's IPO proved that transparency, long-term strategy, and market trust could overcome unconventional methods. Within one year, its stock price tripled. Within three, it had surpassed $500 per share. Google's focus on strong fundamentals, scalable innovation, and disciplined leadership set the stage for one of the most successful public market trajectories in modern tech history.

For investors, the Google IPO became a benchmark for how innovative structures can still deliver robust returns, so long as they're underpinned by credible business models and clear market demand.

CHAPTER 1

UNDERSTANDING MARKET DYNAMICS IN IPOS

IPO activity doesn't occur in a vacuum; it ebbs and flows with broader economic, sectoral, and geopolitical conditions. For both companies and investors, timing an IPO involves more than internal readiness; it requires a clear-eyed view of external forces shaping capital markets.

In bull markets, periods marked by economic expansion, rising equities, and investor optimism, IPO volume typically surges. Companies seek to capitalize on elevated valuations, strong demand, and greater risk appetite among institutional and retail investors. Conversely, in bear markets or during macroeconomic uncertainty, IPO activity often slows. Investors become more selective, pricing becomes more conservative, and companies may delay their offerings to preserve valuation or reduce execution risk.

Sector-specific trends also heavily influence the IPO pipeline. Innovation cycles in technology, biotech, renewable energy, and AI often create IPO clusters, as investor enthusiasm and capital converge around promising new business models. For example, the AI-driven IPO wave in the mid-2020s mirrors the cloud computing and SaaS surge of the early 2010s. Investors who recognize these cycles early and differentiate between durable business models and momentum plays gain an edge in evaluating opportunity and risk.

Geopolitical developments play a subtler but equally powerful role. Events such as the Russia-Ukraine conflict, tensions in the Middle East, and U.S.-China regulatory standoffs can influence investor sentiment, liquidity, and global capital flows. For companies considering a public debut, these variables affect everything from valuation sensitivity to the availability of underwriters and anchor investors. For investors, they shape risk appetite, sector rotation, and the perceived stability of different listing jurisdictions.

Understanding these market dynamics is not about predicting the future; it's about interpreting signals. Elevated inflation may prompt investors to favor cash-generating IPOs over long-duration growth plays. Regulatory tightening in one region may divert IPOs to more favorable markets. Currency fluctuations, interest rate shifts, and capital controls can all affect a company's cost of capital, investor base, and post-listing performance.

For IPO investors, the key is to contextualize each offering within its macro backdrop. Why is this company going public now? What external forces may influence its near-term performance or long-term valuation? Is the timing opportunistic or strategic?

In the end, successful IPO investing is as much about reading the market as it is about reading the prospectus. Economic conditions and global events form the canvas upon which every IPO is painted. The more informed the investor, the clearer the picture.

THE EVOLVING LANDSCAPE OF IPO INVESTING

The IPO landscape has become more dynamic, more global, and significantly more complex. Investors today operate in a radically different environment than even a decade ago, one shaped by accelerated information cycles, technological disruption, and evolving market structures.

Regulatory frameworks continue to shift across jurisdictions, from tightening disclosure requirements in the U.S. to expanding access in emerging markets. Meanwhile, new technologies have transformed the tools investors use to evaluate IPOs. AI-powered analytics, algorithmic trading, and real-time sentiment tracking via social media have blurred the line between institutional strategy and retail intuition.

Commission-free platforms have further democratized participation, empowering retail investors to engage with IPOs more directly, but also exposing them to higher volatility, media-driven hype cycles, and shorter holding horizons. In parallel, institutional investors are leaning more heavily on alternative data, machine learning, and predictive modeling to assess IPO readiness, post-listing performance, and long-term scalability.

For investors navigating this environment, opportunity and risk go hand in hand. On one hand, the increased accessibility and transparency of today's markets offer unprecedented exposure to high-growth sectors and early-stage companies. On the other, the speed of news cycles and the influence of crowd psychology can amplify short-term volatility and obscure fundamental analysis.

Success in this evolving landscape requires both adaptability and discipline. It means knowing when to lean into innovation, and when to step back and scrutinize fundamentals. It involves reading not only the prospectus but also the market context surrounding it: investor sentiment, macro signals, sector rotation, and valuation benchmarks.

Above all, it calls for a long-term perspective. While the tools of IPO investing may be changing, the core principles remain constant: thorough due diligence, thoughtful diversification, and alignment with one's risk tolerance and strategic goals. The investors who thrive in this environment are not those chasing trends but those who can synthesize insight, manage uncertainty, and invest with conviction in the face of noise.

FINAL TAKEAWAYS

IPOs are not simply gateways to public capital; they are strategic inflection points that signal a company's maturity, ambition, and readiness to scale under public scrutiny. For investors, they offer a rare chance to enter early into a company's growth journey, often at a pivotal moment when its narrative is still unfolding and its future is being actively shaped.

From the Dutch East India Company to today's AI-driven disruptors, the IPO has evolved alongside the capital markets themselves, mirroring the changing balance between innovation and regulation, access and accountability, hype and fundamentals. Whether through traditional offerings, direct listings, or SPACs, IPOs remain a powerful reflection of investor sentiment and economic vision.

But opportunity alone is not enough. Navigating today's IPO environment demands adaptability, rigorous analysis, and strategic clarity. Investors must parse signal from noise, distinguish novelty from value, and assess whether a company's public debut aligns with broader market dynamics, and with their own investment philosophy.

In a world defined by volatility and accelerated change, those who approach IPOs with informed curiosity, discipline, and a long-term perspective are best positioned not just to participate in capital markets but to help shape their direction.

CHAPTER 2
Evolution in the Digital Era

EXAMINING THE IMPACT OF TECHNOLOGY ON THE IPO PROCESS

The IPO landscape is continuously evolving, marked by periods of significant transformation that have reshaped the way companies access public markets and how investors participate in them. Historically, the IPO process was a meticulously orchestrated affair, dominated by investment banks and institutional investors. This early era was characterized by an intense reliance on personal networks, physical roadshows, and a somewhat insular market that was challenging for the average retail investor to penetrate.

With the advent of digital technologies, the stage was set for a new chapter in the history of IPOs, one that is far more inclusive and dynamic. From the traditional, somewhat opaque avenues to the public market to the streamlined and transparent process we see today, the metamorphosis of IPOs in the digital era is both fascinating and revolutionary.

Early on, the IPO process was characterized by a level of exclusivity that often left individual investors on the sidelines, with institutional players dominating the landscape. The extensive reliance on the physical roadshows, paper-based documentation, and a select group of underwriters and institutional investors underscored a system that, while effective, was ripe for innovation.

But digital technologies have shattered these old paradigms, ushering in a new era of accessibility, efficiency, and inclusivity in the IPO process.

The democratization of information has been a cornerstone of this transformation. Where once market insights and details on upcoming IPOs were closely monitored by a few select individuals, today's digital platforms offer a wealth of information to a broad audience. This shift has empowered a new generation of investors, equipping them with the tools and data necessary to participate in IPOs that were previously beyond their reach.

Digital trading platforms have played a pivotal role in this evolution. By simplifying the process of participating in IPOs, these platforms have not only opened the doors to a wider range of investors, but they've also introduced a level of efficiency and speed previously unattainable.

Yet, with these advancements come new considerations. The increase in retail investor participation, driven by digital access, introduces new variables into the IPO equation, affecting everything from pricing strategies to post-IPO market performance. As a capital market expert, I view these changes through a lens of cautious optimism. The opportunities presented by digital transformation are vast, but they require a nuanced understanding of market dynamics and a strategic approach to navigating these new platforms.

When reflecting on the digital transformation of IPOs, it's clear that we stand on the cusp of a new era in public market access. The changes we've witnessed are not mere adjustments but a fundamental shift toward a more inclusive and transparent market. For companies considering going public and investors looking to participate in IPOs, the digital age offers unprecedented opportunities.

However, seizing them requires adaptability, strategic foresight, and an in-depth understanding of the ever-evolving digital world.

CASE STUDY: COINBASE - A MILESTONE DIRECT LISTING IN THE CRYPTO INDUSTRY

Overview

In April 2021, Coinbase Global Inc., a leading cryptocurrency exchange, made history as the first major crypto platform to go public via a direct listing on NASDAQ under the ticker symbol "COIN." This event marked a significant moment for the crypto industry, bridging the gap between decentralized digital assets and traditional financial markets. Unlike a traditional initial public offering (IPO), Coinbase opted for a direct listing, allowing existing shareholders to sell their shares directly to the public without raising new capital or involving underwriters.

Digital Relevance

Coinbase's listing highlighted several themes central to the evolution of digital-first public offerings:

Disintermediation: By bypassing investment banks and underwriters, Coinbase avoided hefty fees and ensured full transparency in its valuation process. This approach aligns with the ethos of decentralization inherent in blockchain technology.

Digitally Native Business: As a cryptocurrency exchange founded in 2012, Coinbase operates entirely within the digital economy, offering services such as buying, selling, and trading over 250 cryptocurrencies. Its platform caters to retail and institutional investors, emphasizing accessibility and security.

Market Dynamics: The direct listing mechanism allowed market-based price discovery on the first day of trading. Shares opened at $381, significantly higher than the NASDAQ reference price of $250, and peaked at $429 before closing at $328 on its debut day.

Outcome

Coinbase's initial valuation exceeded $100 billion, underscoring investor enthusiasm for blockchain-native businesses. However, its stock experienced significant volatility in subsequent months due to fluctuations in cryptocurrency prices and broader market conditions. By December 2022, shares hit a low of $31.83 before recovering modestly. This volatility reflects the risks associated with crypto-related businesses, which are closely tied to market sentiment and regulatory developments.

Investor Takeaway

Coinbase's debut reshaped traditional IPO norms by leveraging a direct listing model.

Advantages: The absence of new share issuance prevented dilution of existing equity, while market-driven pricing offered transparency. This model is particularly suited for companies that do not need immediate capital but seek liquidity for insiders.

Risks: Direct listings expose investors to heightened volatility due to the lack of institutional support typically associated with IPOs. Additionally, regulatory uncertainties surrounding cryptocurrencies can impact trading volumes and profitability.

Market Significance: Coinbase's listing demonstrated growing investor appetite for exposure to blockchain-native businesses, signaling increased mainstream acceptance of cryptocurrencies as an asset class.

Conclusion

Coinbase's direct listing was a landmark event that showcased how digital-first companies are redefining public market entry strategies. While it underscored the potential of blockchain-based businesses, it also highlighted the inherent risks tied to crypto market volatility and regulatory challenges. As such, Coinbase remains emblematic of the opportunities and complexities in integrating decentralized finance into traditional markets.

THE PRE-DIGITAL IPO PROCESS

The traditional IPO process, before the advent of digital technologies, was a complex and highly structured endeavor that served as the primary gateway for companies seeking to enter the public markets. This method involved several key stages, starting with the selection of investment banks to serve as underwriters. These institutions were tasked with a critical role: To determine the offering price of the IPO, ensure regulatory compliance, and ultimately sell the shares to investors. The process was characterized by its reliance on a network, with investment banks leveraging their relationships to market the IPO to institutional investors and select high-net-worth individuals through a series of in-person roadshows. These roadshows were pivotal, providing a platform for company executives to present their business models, financial health, and growth prospects directly to potential investors.

However, the traditional IPO process was not without its limitations. One significant drawback was its lack of accessibility for the average retail investor. The heavy reliance on institutional investors and the exclusive nature of the roadshows meant that information and participation were largely restricted to a select group of market participants. This exclusivity not only limited the potential investor base for companies but also restricted the broader market's ability to engage with, and invest in, new public entities. Furthermore, the time-consuming nature of the roadshow circuit, and the extensive regulatory and documentation requirements, made the IPO process costly and lengthy, posing additional challenges for companies seeking public capital.

Investment banks and underwriters played a central role in the pre-digital era, acting as the gatekeepers of the IPO process. Their expertise in market analysis, valuation, and regulatory compliance was indispensable in guiding companies desiring to go public. However, this dependence on investment banks also meant that the IPO process was heavily intermediated, with these institutions exerting significant influence over the timing, pricing, and distribution of IPO shares. While this model ensured a certain level of quality and rigor in the offerings brought to market, it also concentrated power and information in the hands of a few, often leading to problematic issues of transparency and market efficiency.

When I view the pre-digital IPO process from my perspective and experience in the capital markets, it's clear that while effective in facilitating public offerings, it was a system in desperate need of innovation. The limitations of accessibility, efficiency, and especially openness highlighted the need for a more inclusive and streamlined approach. The subsequent digital transformation of the IPO process, driven by technological advancements and regulatory changes, is addressing these challenges, opening up new pathways for companies to access public capital and myriad investors to participate in the growth of these companies. This evolution into a more democratized and efficient market is a welcome development, signaling a shift toward greater market participation and more vibrant public investment.

TECHNOLOGICAL DISRUPTIONS IN THE IPO FRAMEWORK

The launch of electronic trading platforms represented a watershed moment for the IPO process, fundamentally transforming the mechanics of securities trading and the approach companies take toward entering the public market. During my time in the capital markets, I have witnessed the profound effects of these platforms on the IPO ecosystem. Initially, these platforms made the transaction process more efficient, drastically cutting both the time and costs associated with trading securities. This leap in technological advancement didn't just boost market efficiency; it also increased the overall liquidity of the stock market, rendering it a more appealing and accessible option for companies considering an IPO.

Furthermore, electronic trading platforms dismantled the traditional barriers that had restricted IPO participation to a narrow circle of institutional investors and individuals of significant wealth. By opening up market access to a wider range of participants, these platforms have been instrumental in creating many new investment opportunities. This evolution has allowed a more varied pool of investors to partake in IPOs, broadening the prospective investor base for companies aiming to go public. The initial impact of this development was monumental, heralding a new epoch of market participation and setting the stage for ongoing innovations within the IPO process.

From a regulatory standpoint, the JOBS Act played a pivotal role, easing regulatory constraints and carving new paths within our securities laws to aid in capital formation for smaller enterprises. The enactment of the JOBS Act marked a significant step toward facilitating this process, underscoring the government's recognition of the necessity for technological and regulatory adaptation.

The proliferation of the Internet has significantly boosted the access for all investors to market information, a development I regard as among the most crucial in the contemporary capital market financial landscape. Before the Internet's widespread adoption, obtaining details on forthcoming IPOs and the financial well-being of companies was a daunting task for the average investor. The internet revolutionized this, offering a wealth of data and analytical tools once reserved solely for industry professionals. This shift toward openness has not only empowered retail investors, enabling more informed IPO investment decisions, but it has also led to a more transparent market environment, continuously challenging and diminishing information asymmetry.

The impact of the Internet in leveling the investment playing field has been profound, compelling companies and their underwriters to adopt practices that are more transparent and favorable to investors. As an expert in this arena, I have observed how this increased accessibility to information has fostered more participatory and informed market dynamics, significantly contributing to the health and success of the capital markets. Looking forward, the ongoing technological evolution is expected to further refine and transform the IPO process, rendering it more accessible, efficient, and fair for all participants in the market.

CHAPTER 2

ONLINE PLATFORMS AND ACCESS TO IPOS

The integration of online brokers into the IPO distribution model represents a paradigm shift, transforming access to public offerings in ways that have significantly broadened opportunities for the investor. Speaking from decades of experience as an IPO advisor, I've seen this evolution, not just as a facilitation of wider participation but as a critical step toward making the IPO process more efficient. Platforms like SoFi Invest, Robinhood, and Webull have been at the forefront of this change, each contributing uniquely to opening IPOs to a wide diversity of investors (though it is important to note that while these platforms have democratized access by allowing retail investors to participate in IPOs traditionally dominated by institutions, they have also faced criticism over risks such as speculative behavior and lack of investor education). These platforms and their benefits are discussed in deeper detail in chapter 8.

From my vantage point, the role of online platforms in reshaping the IPO distribution model is profound. They not only facilitate direct access to IPOs for retail investors but also contribute to a more dynamic and participatory market environment. This shift is indicative of a larger trend toward the capital markets offering unprecedented opportunities for investors and new considerations for companies preparing to go public. In sum, the digital transformation of the IPO distribution model, spearheaded by platforms like SoFi, Robinhood, and Webull, marks a significant milestone toward a more equitable and accessible financial market.

CASE STUDY: ROBINHOOD – DEMOCRATIZING IPO ACCESS

Robinhood, a leading commission-free trading platform, made headlines in 2021 by offering shares of its own IPO directly to its users, democratizing the process of investing in an IPO for the first time. Traditionally, IPO shares were allocated primarily to institutional investors, but Robinhood's decision to offer shares to its retail base marked a significant shift in the IPO distribution model.

While the platform's IPO Access initiative was met with mixed reactions, with some questioning the risks for retail investors, it ultimately set a precedent for future IPOs. The Robinhood IPO itself had a rocky start, with the stock price dropping significantly post-offer, but the move represented a larger trend of increasing accessibility for retail investors to participate in high-profile IPOs.

Investor Takeaway

Robinhood's IPO Access platform highlights the growing trend of retail inclusion in the IPO market and demonstrates the potential for new platforms to reshape how IPOs are accessed by investors, particularly those who were previously excluded from such opportunities.

REGULATORY RESPONSES TO TECHNOLOGICAL ADVANCEMENTS

The intersection of technology and regulatory oversight in the IPO process has increasingly become a focal point for the Securities and Exchange Commission (SEC) and the Financial Industry Regulatory Authority (FINRA). As a leading industry participant with extensive experience in the nuances of IPOs and regulatory compliance, I've observed firsthand the challenges and opportunities that technology presents, especially for retail investors. The evolution of digital platforms facilitating broader access to IPOs necessitates a dynamic regulatory approach to ensure market integrity and protect investor interests.

The SEC and FINRA have been proactive in addressing the complexities introduced by digital innovations in the IPO process. This includes the adaptation of regulations to manage the risks associated with increased retail investor participation and the use of online platforms for IPO access. For instance, amendments to rules regarding the marketing and communication surrounding IPOs reflect an understanding of the broader reach and impact of digital platforms. These regulatory bodies have also focused on ensuring that retail investors receive the same level of information as institutional participants. The aim is to create a level playing field where informed decision-making is supported by comprehensive disclosures and fair access to all investment opportunities.

The SEC and FINRA have implemented regulations that support the entry of smaller companies into the public market while ensuring investor protection. The JOBS Act is a prime example, reducing reporting and compliance burdens for emerging growth companies (EGCs) and facilitating their public offerings. Additionally, FINRA's rules around crowdfunding and online capital-raising activities have provided structured pathways for smaller companies to access public capital through digital means. These regulations not only aid in the democratization of investing but also ensure that the market remains fair for all participants.

Moreover, the regulatory landscape continues to evolve in response to new technological challenges, including issues of cybersecurity, data privacy, and the potential for market manipulation through social media and other digital channels. The SEC and FINRA are actively engaging with these challenges, issuing guidance, and adapting regulations to protect the market and its participants from emerging risks.

From my perspective, it's clear that the regulatory responses from the SEC and FINRA to technological advancements are crucial for maintaining a robust and inclusive market. As technology continues to evolve, so, too, will the regulatory frameworks that govern the IPO process. The ongoing dialogue between regulators, industry participants, and investors will be vital in navigating the future sphere of IPOs. Ensuring that regulations keep pace with innovation without stifling growth or limiting access to the market will be a delicate balance but essential for the continued health and growth of the public markets.

THE RISE OF ALTERNATIVE PUBLIC OFFERINGS AND THE ROLE OF SOCIAL MEDIA

Direct listings present a compelling alternative by allowing companies to list their shares directly on a stock exchange without raising new capital through underwriters. This approach not only bypasses the hefty fees associated with traditional IPOs, but it also offers a more market-driven price discovery process, reducing the potential for the initial pop and subsequent volatility often seen in IPOs. The success stories of companies like Spotify and Slack, which opted for direct listings, underscore the viability and attractiveness of this method, especially for well-capitalized firms that prioritize direct market access and shareholder equality.

Simultaneously, the digital age has ushered in the era of social media, profoundly impacting investor behavior and IPO marketing strategies. Social media platforms have created information dissemination, enabling companies to directly engage with a broad audience of potential investors. This direct line of communication allows for a more nuanced and dynamic marketing approach, extending beyond traditional roadshows to include interactive Q&A sessions, live broadcasts, and viral content.

However, this new frontier also presents challenges, as the rapid spread of information (and misinformation) can significantly influence investor sentiment and market dynamics. Companies and regulators alike are navigating these waters carefully, seeking to leverage the power of social media while ensuring accuracy and compliance with disclosure regulations.

The rise of alternative public offerings, the influence of social media, and the role of crowdfunding are reshaping how companies approach going public, offering new opportunities and challenges in equal measure. As the market continues to evolve, so, too, will the strategies companies employ to access public capital.

CASE STUDY: BEYOND MEAT - THE ROLE OF SOCIAL MEDIA IN IPOS

Beyond Meat's 2019 IPO is a prime example of how social media can amplify investor enthusiasm and create volatility in the IPO market. The company's focus on plant-based meat alternatives resonated with consumers and investors alike, but it was the social media buzz, particularly on platforms like Twitter and Instagram, that truly accelerated demand for shares.

Beyond Meat's stock soared on its first day of trading, but this rapid rise was also followed by significant volatility. In the months following the IPO, the stock price fluctuated wildly, highlighting the potential risks of hype-driven IPOs, particularly when retail investors are heavily influenced by social media and online marketing.

Investor Takeaway

Beyond Meat's IPO underscores the importance of discerning fundamentals from hype and the risks posed by the influence of social media on stock prices. For investors, it's a reminder to evaluate companies carefully and avoid getting swept up in the excitement.

BLOCKCHAIN AND THE FUTURE OF IPOS

Blockchain technology is poised to revolutionize the IPO process and securities trading, introducing levels of efficiency, transparency, and security previously unattainable. Within the capital markets sphere, I foresee blockchain's decentralized and immutable ledger fundamentally altering how securities are issued, traded, and recorded.

This technology has the potential to streamline the IPO process by automating many of the regulatory and compliance requirements through smart contracts, significantly reducing the time and cost associated with public offerings. Furthermore, blockchain could enhance accountability and trust in securities trading, providing a real-time, verifiable record of transactions accessible to all market participants. This could diminish the likelihood of fraud and errors, ensuring a more secure and reliable market environment. Undoubtedly, the adoption of blockchain in securities trading and the IPO process represents a forward leap in our quest for a more efficient financial system.

In the realm of digital-era financing, Initial Coin Offerings (ICOs) and Security Token Offerings (STOs) have emerged as novel alternatives to traditional IPOs, leveraging blockchain technology to expand access to capital. ICOs, while initially popular for their ease of access and lack of regulatory oversight, have faced scrutiny due to instances of fraud and market manipulation. In response,

STOs have risen in prominence, offering a regulated and more secure means of raising capital through the issuance of digital tokens that represent ownership in real-world assets. These digital offerings embody the convergence of traditional financial mechanisms with the innovative potential of blockchain, suggesting a future where capital formation is accessible and regulated. As these digital-era analogs to IPOs continue to evolve, they are likely to play a significant role in reshaping future IPOs, challenging traditional models with their efficiency, accessibility, and global reach.

DATA ANALYTICS AND AI IN DECISION-MAKING

The integration of big data and artificial intelligence (AI) into the decision-making processes surrounding IPOs marks a significant evolution in how companies approach the public market. I've recently witnessed the transformative power of these technologies in optimizing IPO timing, pricing, and investor targeting in the capital markets. Leveraging vast datasets, AI algorithms can analyze market conditions, investor sentiment, and historical IPO outcomes to guide companies in choosing the most opportune moment to go public. Furthermore, AI-driven insights can refine pricing strategies, ensuring that they align with current market dynamics and investor expectations. This precision in timing and pricing is invaluable, as it can significantly impact the initial and long-term success of an IPO. Moreover, AI's ability to segment and identify potential investors based on their investment history and preferences allows for more targeted and effective marketing strategies, ensuring that the offering resonates with the most receptive audience.

Looking to the future, the implications of AI-driven analytics for IPO success prediction are profound. As these technologies continue to advance, their predictive capabilities will become increasingly sophisticated, offering more nuanced and accurate forecasts of IPO performance. This progression promises to not only enhance the efficiency and effectiveness of IPOs but also to broaden access to these investment opportunities. Smaller companies, which may previously have been deterred by the uncertainty and complexity of going public, could find AI-driven analytics a game-changer, enabling them to navigate the IPO process with greater confidence and strategic insight. For investors, the use of AI in IPOs could mean more data-backed investment opportunities, minimizing speculation and promoting informed decision-making. As we move forward, the integration of big data and AI into the IPO landscape is likely to redefine success in the public markets, making it a more data-driven, precise, and inclusive arena for companies and investors alike.

THE ONGOING EVOLUTION OF IPOS

Incorporating the perspective of opportunity for investors into the ongoing evolution of IPOs adds another layer of significance to the transformative impact of technology on the capital markets. This era of innovation not only opens up new avenues for companies to access public markets, but it also presents unprecedented opportunities for investors. The easier access through online platforms and the advent of alternative public offerings like direct listings, ICOs (initial coin offering), and STOs (security token offering), have expanded investment possibilities. Investors now have a broader spectrum of opportunities at their fingertips, ranging from traditional equity offerings to blockchain-based securities, each carrying its unique risk and reward profile.

Furthermore, the integration of advanced technologies such as AI and data analytics into the IPO process offers tools to investors for deeper market analysis and investment decision-making. These technologies can provide predictive insights into IPO performance, market trends, and investment strategies, enabling institutional and retail investors to make more informed choices. The potential for blockchain to add a layer of security and transparency to securities trading could further enhance investor confidence, making participation in IPOs and other public offerings more appealing.

FINAL TAKEAWAYS

The future of IPOs, shaped by technological innovation, holds immense promise for current and new investors willing to navigate this evolving system. As opportunities for investment diversify and become more accessible, the role of investor education and financial literacy becomes increasingly critical. Investors equipped with the knowledge to understand and leverage these new tools and platforms will be well-positioned to capitalize on the opportunities presented by the digital transformation of the IPO process. The ongoing evolution of IPOs not only signifies a shift in how companies go public; additionally, it heralds a new era of investment opportunity, characterized by greater accessibility, enhanced transparency, and the potential for significant returns. Embracing this future requires a proactive approach to learning and adaptation, ensuring that investors of all types can participate fully in the exciting developments unfolding in the capital markets.

CHAPTER 3

The Importance of IPOs in the Economy

Imagine standing amidst the bustling crowd at the New York Stock Exchange or Nasdaq on the morning of a major IPO. The air is electric, charged with anticipation and the collective buzz of years of planning and countless conversations about market potentials and the future of the company. Around you, financial analysts, reporters, and traders discuss the monumental day, a pivotal transition for emerging companies making their public debut. On the digital screens, logos of new public entities appear prominently, each symbolizing significant corporate and economic transformations.

This scene isn't just a financial milestone; it's a cultural and economic turning point. IPOs are more than share issuances; they are strategic events that shape capital markets, fuel company growth, and drive broader economic progress. They invite thousands of public investors to partake in a company's future and reflect the vitality of our financial system.

Understanding the role IPOs play in the economy provides valuable insight for investors. According to a 2021 study by the *Kauffman Foundation*, IPOs are responsible for an average of 822 new jobs per company in the first year alone. Likewise, research from Stanford University found that companies boost their patent filings by 50 percent in the five years after going public, a clear sign of increased innovation.

These events aren't merely about selling shares; they are about crafting legacies and catapulting ideas into wider realms of influence. They offer companies the capital needed to scale operations, enter new markets, and accelerate product development. For investors, IPOs can provide early access to transformative growth stories.

By understanding the importance of IPOs, we gain insights into the mechanics of markets and the rhythm of economic cycles. Let's explore how these monumental events shape the economy, influence lives, and continue to redefine the boundaries of what is possible in business and beyond.

On September 14, 2023, Arm Holdings went public on the NASDAQ under the ticker symbol ARM, raising $4.87 billion in one of the most anticipated IPOs of the year. The offering, which valued the company at approximately $54.5 billion, underscored the market's strong demand for semiconductor and AI-related technologies. This event exemplifies how IPOs not only raise capital but also capture public interest and shape economic trends, particularly in the rapidly evolving AI and chip industries.

ECONOMIC GROWTH THROUGH CAPITAL INFUSION

A successful IPO reshapes industries, catalyzes innovation, and propels economic momentum on a global scale. When a company transitions from private to public ownership, the influx of capital enables a fundamental shift, not just within the company itself but across financial markets, investor networks, and the broader economy.

At its core, an IPO redistributes financial returns across a broader, more diverse investor base. What was once the exclusive domain of venture capitalists and private equity firms becomes an opportunity for institutional and retail investors alike. This democratization of capital fosters widespread participation in wealth creation, ensuring that economic growth is not confined to a select few but is instead shared among a broader spectrum of market participants.

The effects of an IPO ripple far beyond the trading floor. These public offerings fuel corporate expansion, enable aggressive R&D investment, and provide the financial stability necessary for long-term strategic planning. Companies that successfully go public gain access to deeper pools of capital, allowing them to scale operations, explore new markets, and accelerate product innovation. This, in turn, stimulates job creation, strengthens supply chains, and supports ancillary industries that rely on the growth of public enterprises.

We can see IPOs as more than just financial transactions; they serve as barometers of economic health and investor sentiment. In bullish markets, a surge in IPO activity signals confidence, reinforcing a cycle of investment and expansion. Conversely, in uncertain times, companies may delay their public debut, wary of market volatility and shifting investor risk appetites. The very act of a company going public or choosing not to tells a broader story about the current state of the economy, industry trends, and future expectations.

Beyond the immediate financial implications, IPOs play a vital role in economic renewal. As emerging industries gain prominence through public offerings, they often surpass older, less adaptive sectors, driving an evolution of economic priorities. Take, for example, the rise of technology IPOs in the past two decades. Companies like Amazon, Google, and Tesla did not merely go public; they redefined entire industries, displacing traditional players and setting new benchmarks for innovation and efficiency.

The IPO process facilitates this creative destruction, allowing capital to flow into dynamic, high-growth sectors that push the economy forward.

As new technologies reshape market expectations, IPOs increasingly serve as launch pads for transformative sectors. Nowhere is this more evident than in artificial intelligence.

CASE STUDY: MODERNA – IPO-FUNDED INNOVATION THAT CHANGED GLOBAL HEALTH

When Moderna went public in December 2018 (NASDAQ: MRNA), the company was still a clinical-stage biotech firm with no approved products and a novel but unproven mRNA platform. Its $604 million IPO was one of the largest biotech offerings at the time, raising capital critical to advancing its pipeline.

Less than two years later, that same platform enabled Moderna to become one of the first companies in the world to develop a COVID-19 vaccine in record time. The IPO proceeds helped fund not only the vaccine's development but also the build-out of manufacturing infrastructure necessary to scale production globally.

This case exemplifies how IPOs fuel breakthrough innovation by unlocking the capital needed to commercialize transformational science. Moderna's public listing provided transparency, accountability, and long-term investor alignment elements that allowed the company to act quickly and responsibly at a moment of global urgency.

CHAPTER 3

AI: THE NEW FRONTIER SHAPING IPO MARKETS

The IPO landscape is undergoing a material shift as artificial intelligence (AI) emerges as the defining force of the next decade. Morgan Stanley anticipates 10–15 tech IPOs driven by AI's transformative potential, with companies like CoreWeave (targeting a $35 billion valuation) and Databricks ($62 billion private valuation) leading the charge in 2025. AI-native startups are projected to dominate funding momentum, with Sapphire Ventures predicting many will surpass $50M in annual recurring revenue (ARR). This aligns with EY's research, which found 97 percent of senior leaders report positive ROI from AI investments, fueling a projected $1 trillion in global AI spending by 2030.

AI is projected to contribute up to $13 trillion to global economic output by 2030, according to McKinsey. That's a 1.2 percent annual uplift to global GDP, driven by breakthroughs in productivity, automation, and intelligent systems across industries.

The emergence of AI is set to amplify this transformative effect of IPOs, ushering in a new era of economic renewal and innovation. AI-driven companies going public are not just raising capital; they are reshaping entire industries and redefining the very nature of work and productivity. By 2030, AI could potentially deliver an additional economic output of around $13 trillion, boosting global GDP by about 1.2 percent a year. This growth will be driven by AI's ability to enhance productivity across various sectors, from manufacturing to healthcare and financial services.

For investors, the implication is clear: IPOs in AI aren't just about tech exposure; they're about gaining early access to the next wave of industrial transformation.

As AI-driven companies reshape industries and fuel economic growth, the role of IPOs transcends capital generation. These offerings enable the scaling of transformative technologies and introduce a framework of corporate governance vital for long-term sustainability. The transition from private to public status compels these disruptive companies to adopt rigorous standards of transparency and accountability, aligning technological advancement with ethical business practices and investor protection.

Going public aligns corporate futures with shareholder interests. Public companies must operate with greater accountability and strategic discipline. Investor relations and market perception become essential to strategy, reinforcing a culture of responsibility.

Ultimately, IPOs inject vitality into capital markets, foster economic inclusion, and set the stage for future innovation. These moments represent more than the ringing of the opening bell; they mark the beginning of new chapters in corporate history, new opportunities for investors, and new possibilities for industries poised to define the future.

CASE STUDY: C3.AI - RIDING THE AI WAVE INTO THE PUBLIC MARKETS

C3.ai, one of the first enterprise AI software firms to go public, listed on the NYSE in December 2020 under the ticker AI. Priced at $42 per share, the company's valuation soared as its stock more than doubled on the first day of trading, fueled by investor excitement over artificial intelligence and big data analytics.

However, the stock quickly fell from its highs in the months following its debut, highlighting the volatility that often accompanies high-profile technology IPOs. Despite market fluctuations, the listing enabled C3.ai to expand its offerings, attract key enterprise clients, and continue investing in platform development.

This case illustrates both the promise and the hype surrounding AI-related IPOs. Investors must weigh the long-term potential of disruptive technologies against the speculative nature of early-stage valuations, particularly in sectors where growth precedes profitability.

CATALYSTS FOR INNOVATION

IPOs serve as a launchpad for industry leadership, technological breakthroughs, and global competitiveness. The capital raised through an IPO allows companies to fund ambitious R&D initiatives and scale their operations rapidly.

Tesla's IPO proceeds were instrumental in expanding its electric vehicle and battery technology, reshaping the global auto industry. Amazon's IPO helped build its e-commerce infrastructure and, later, its cloud computing empire.

Biotech offers another compelling example. A 2023 study from BIO revealed that 67 percent of new FDA-approved drugs in the past decade originated from companies that went public within fifteen years of approval. This underscores how IPO capital can translate directly into life-saving innovation.

You may argue that IPO capital is a one-time boost. On the contrary, it fuels a continuous cycle of reinvention. Companies like NIO, a Chinese EV manufacturer, have used IPO proceeds to fund R&D, scale production, and compete globally.

Public companies must disclose financial strategies and long-term objectives, ensuring that innovation aligns with investor expectations. This transparency encourages efficient capital allocation and responsible growth.

The wealth generated through IPOs also fosters entrepreneurial ecosystems. It inspires startups to pursue bold ideas, knowing that the public markets may one day provide the resources to scale globally. IPOs do not just create shareholder value; they power economic advancement and societal impact.

CASE STUDY: AIRBNB – EXPANDING RETAIL ACCESS TO IPOS

Airbnb's December 2020 IPO was one of the most anticipated of the decade. Priced at $68 per share, the stock opened at $146, more than doubling on its first day of trading. The dramatic surge raised questions about underpricing, with billions in potential capital left on the table.

But Airbnb's IPO was notable for another reason: its accessibility. Through platforms like Robinhood and SoFi, thousands of retail investors were able to participate in the IPO at the offering price, not just post-market.

This marked a shift in how IPOs are distributed, with increased transparency and participation beyond traditional institutional channels. While the price action was volatile in the months following the IPO, the listing democratized access to one of Silicon Valley's biggest success stories, aligning with the broader push to open up capital markets to everyday investors.

ENHANCING THE DYNAMICS OF CAPITAL MARKETS

IPOs inject vitality into capital markets by expanding liquidity, deepening market participation, and offering fresh diversification opportunities for investors. By listing new companies, they grow the universe of investable assets.

Increased liquidity improves market efficiency. For institutional investors, it provides flexibility in managing large positions. For retail investors, it lowers transaction costs and narrows bid-ask spreads.

Airbnb's IPO, for example, provided access to a company that had previously been the domain of private equity. This broadened public ownership and enabled a wider array of investors to benefit from the company's growth.

For institutions, IPOs provide an avenue to allocate capital toward high-growth opportunities, while for retail investors, they mark an entry point into companies previously beyond reach.

New listings also invite more analyst coverage, media attention, and investor education, enriching the informational landscape of public markets. As more data becomes available, investors can make better-informed decisions.

FINAL TAKEAWAYS

Ultimately, IPOs contribute to a more inclusive and dynamic financial system. They enhance transparency, improve price discovery, and ensure capital flows to where it can drive innovation and progress. In doing so, IPOs shape not only financial portfolios but the future of industries and economies alike.

CASE STUDY: SAUDI ARAMCO - THE LARGEST IPO IN HISTORY

In December 2019, Saudi Aramco raised $25.6 billion in the world's largest IPO to date, listing on the Tadawul (Saudi

Stock Exchange). Unlike many IPOs driven by innovation or growth capital needs, Aramco's listing was part of a broader economic diversification strategy under Saudi Arabia's Vision 2030 plan.

The IPO highlighted the role of public markets not just in raising funds but in reshaping global economic narratives. While the offering was largely domestic, it generated intense international scrutiny and recalibrated global capital flows toward the Middle East.

Though not a U.S.-based IPO, Aramco's listing underscores how public markets can reflect geopolitical ambition and national economic strategy in addition to company-specific growth stories.

CHAPTER 4

IPO Investment Stages and Considerations

Investing in IPOs can be rewarding and complex. While some IPOs have delivered exponential returns, many underperform the broader market in their first year of trading. A successful IPO investment strategy requires more than enthusiasm; it demands a structured approach grounded in diligence, timing, and discipline. This involves identifying promising pre-IPO opportunities, evaluating the pricing and demand signals at the time of the IPO, and actively managing the investment once the company begins trading publicly. Each stage introduces its own risks and decision points, from opaque private valuations to early volatility and insider lock-up expirations. For investors, the ability to navigate these stages with clarity and conviction can make the difference between capturing outsized gains and absorbing costly missteps. This chapter explores the full IPO investment journey, providing a practical roadmap for approaching these opportunities with strategic foresight and investor-grade rigor.

STAGE 1: PRE-IPO INVESTING & PREPARATION

Investing in a company before it goes public presents the possibility of outsized returns, often before the broader market has access. However, that potential upside comes with heightened uncertainty, limited transparency, and the need for rigorous due diligence. Pre-IPO opportunities are often tightly held by institutional investors, venture capitalists, and insiders. For individual investors to succeed in this early-stage arena, they must not only find access points but also apply institutional-grade scrutiny to every deal.

Identifying the right pre-IPO companies requires a keen understanding of multiple factors: valuation, leadership, market dynamics, and exit potential. Valuation benchmarks are essential, as investors must compare the company's pricing to sector averages and recent public comps. Industries like technology and biotechnology often command premium multiples due to their innovation-driven growth, but high valuations can mask operational fragility.

The experience and track record of a company's leadership team also play a crucial role in determining long-term outcomes. Companies led by CEOs with prior IPO or public company experience tend to perform more predictably in the transition to the public markets. Likewise, a strong, independent board helps reduce governance risks and supports investor confidence through post-IPO volatility.

A company's market position and competitive strength are equally important. Key metrics, such as revenue growth, CAC-to-LTV ratios, and operational scalability, help investors evaluate whether the business can sustain performance after listing. Barriers to entry, such as intellectual property, regulatory protection, or entrenched customer relationships, are additional indicators of long-term viability.

That said, even the most promising private companies present risk. Liquidity constraints are a major issue. Unlike publicly traded stocks, pre-IPO shares are illiquid and may remain so for years. Investors must assess whether their capital can be tied up for extended periods or explore secondary market platforms that offer partial flexibility.

Valuation uncertainty is another serious challenge. Many late-stage startups have inflated private valuations that do not translate in the public markets. Historical data shows that a significant proportion of IPOs—ranging from approximately 30 percent to over 60 percent—underperform relative to market benchmarks within one to five years after issuance. Investors can protect themselves by conducting relative valuation analysis, examining revenue multiples, and looking at precedent transactions.

The problem is compounded by limited access to reliable financial data. Information asymmetry is common, especially for retail investors, and can result in poor decision-making if not addressed. Mitigating this requires leaning on verified financial disclosures, audited statements, and reputable SEC-registered investment platforms.

Regulatory risk should also not be overlooked. Some pre-IPO companies operate in jurisdictions or sectors with weak compliance frameworks, making them vulnerable to enforcement action. Unregistered securities, exaggerated claims, or vague ownership structures have tripped up many unprepared investors. Focusing on companies with transparent governance and a strong compliance history is essential.

Finally, timing and market cycles can derail even well-structured IPO plans. In 2024, nearly 60 percent of late-stage startups delayed their listings due to adverse market conditions. Investors must factor in external headwinds and maintain a long-term horizon. Diversification across asset types and IPO timelines can help balance the risk.

In short, pre-IPO investing can be a powerful strategy, but only when approached with discipline, access to quality data, and a readiness to hold through volatility. For investors who do the work upfront, the payoff can be significant.

But the margin for error is narrow, and the penalties for overlooking risk are steep.

The following case study illustrates how even the most promising late-stage startups can challenge investor expectations in the pre-IPO phase:

CASE STUDY: STRIPE'S ELUSIVE IPO AND PRE-IPO INVESTING RISKS

Stripe, the global payments giant, became one of the most anticipated IPOs of the decade without ever going public. By 2021, Stripe had raised over $2 billion in private capital and achieved a $95 billion valuation, making it the most valuable privately held startup in the U.S. For pre-IPO investors, this valuation represented immense opportunity and significant risk.

In early 2023, Stripe raised another $6.5 billion but at a $50 billion valuation, nearly half its prior peak. The reduced valuation was part of a broader trend of declining tech startup valuations during that period. This dramatic markdown forced many institutional investors, including Fidelity and Tiger Global, to write down their holdings. The company cited employee stock compensation and balance sheet flexibility as reasons for the raise, but the valuation cut reflected broader tech market corrections.

Pre-IPO investors faced limited liquidity, uncertain exit timing, and valuation volatility. While Stripe's fundamentals remained strong (annual revenue reportedly exceeded $12 billion), the company's delay in listing underscored a key risk: IPO timelines are unpredictable, and late-stage private markets can overprice growth.

Investor Takeaway

Even high-quality companies carry pre-IPO risk. Without public market pricing, investors must be disciplined in assessing valuation, liquidity constraints, and sector cycles. Stripe's case highlights the importance of patience, diversification, and skepticism when investing in pre-IPO unicorns.

STAGE 2: IPO EXECUTION

Once a company enters the IPO stage, investor scrutiny shifts from long-term potential to short-term execution. This is a critical inflection point where pricing decisions, market sentiment, and allocation structures intersect, often in unpredictable ways. The IPO execution phase is not just about access; it's about interpreting signals under pressure and acting with precision.

Pricing and demand signals provide early insight into the market's expectations. The quality of the underwriters, especially bulge-bracket firms, can significantly impact demand, as their involvement often attracts institutional capital. Oversubscription rates, when demand exceeds share supply, tend to drive first-day gains and signal investor enthusiasm. On the other hand, if the offering is repriced downward before launch or if allocations increase suddenly, it may indicate weak interest or valuation push-back from the market.

The IPO roadshow is a crucial moment in the execution timeline. These presentations are where institutional investors interact with management, probe the financials, and test the company's story. While these sessions are not typically available to retail investors, their influence on institutional sentiment can often predict early price movement. For everyday investors, tracking media commentary, analyst previews, and underwriter behavior offers clues into how the roadshow is being received.

Access remains one of the biggest challenges for retail investors. Most high-demand IPOs reserve over 80 percent of allocations for institutions (although, allocation percentages depend on regulatory frameworks and market practices). As a result, individual investors often receive small allocations or must enter in the aftermarket, when prices have already adjusted. One strategy is to open accounts with full-service brokers that are part of the underwriting syndicate. Another is to monitor pre-listing activity in the secondary market or participate through IPO-focused ETFs that offer fractional exposure.

Before the stock can debut, the SEC must approve the company's S-1 filing, which includes extensive financial and risk disclosures. While not written with investors in mind, the S-1 is a powerful source of insight. Investors should look for discrepancies between the narrative in the roadshow and the details in the filing. Areas to examine include customer concentration, use of proceeds, adjusted EBITDA metrics, and potential legal or regulatory liabilities. A mismatch between the company's pitch and its paperwork is often a red flag.

This phase also comes with significant behavioral risk. The fear of missing out (FOMO), especially in high-profile IPOs, can lead investors to chase early price surges without proper analysis. Overconfidence bias may drive assumptions that every IPO will replicate the success of companies like Google or Amazon, ignoring that most IPOs underperform after their first year. Herd mentality and social proof can intensify these tendencies, as can confirmation bias when investors become emotionally attached to a company's story.

To avoid these pitfalls, investors should set clear valuation boundaries before IPO day. Ask: How does the IPO price compare to public peers? Is the business model scalable? What are the realistic growth levers? One underappreciated signal is insider selling; if executives are cashing out large amounts on day one, it could suggest skepticism about long-term performance.

Ultimately, IPO execution is not just a moment of excitement; it's a moment of truth. It reveals how a private-market story withstands the scrutiny of public-market discipline. For investors, maintaining a steady hand, a sharp analytical lens, and an unemotional decision process can turn a hype-fueled frenzy into a well-timed opportunity.

Instacart's IPO in 2023 provides a real-world example of how IPO pricing strategy and market sentiment intersect in the execution phase:

CASE STUDY: INSTACART'S IPO – A REPRICING IN REAL-TIME

In September 2023, Instacart went public under the ticker CART, marking a long-awaited debut for the grocery delivery platform. Priced at $30 per share, Instacart's IPO was viewed as a bellwether for the post-pandemic tech market. Yet behind the scenes, its valuation journey revealed the complexities of IPO execution.

At its peak in 2021, Instacart was valued at $39 billion in the private markets. By the time it was listed, that figure had fallen to $10 billion. To ensure demand, Instacart relied on prominent institutional backers, including Sequoia and PepsiCo (which purchased $175 million in shares), while leaving room for a greenshoe option to stabilize trading.

Shares closed up 12 percent on day one but quickly retreated. Within weeks, the stock dropped below its IPO price, raising concerns about long-term profitability, competition from DoorDash, and declining order volumes.

Investor Takeaway

The IPO execution phase demands careful reading of market signals. A downward valuation revision may secure a successful listing, but it also reflects shifting investor sentiment. Retail investors should scrutinize pre-IPO pricing trends and anchor investments to fundamentals, not headlines.

STAGE 3: POST-IPO MANAGEMENT

The IPO may mark the end of a company's private life, but for investors, it's just the beginning of a critical evaluation phase. Once public, a stock enters a new arena, one where price discovery, market sentiment, and operational performance are tested in real-time. Successful post-IPO management is about discipline, data, and the ability to separate hype from fundamentals.

Stock price volatility is common in the early months following an IPO. With limited public float, modest shifts in sentiment can produce dramatic price swings. One key inflection point is the lock-up expiration—typically around 180 days after listing—when insiders are first permitted to sell shares. These events often lead to downward pressure on the stock, especially if early backers rush to exit. For investors, heavy insider selling post-lock-up may signal a lack of long-term conviction.

Financial reporting becomes the lifeblood of investor insight. Once public, companies are required to file quarterly (10-Q) and annual (10-K) reports. These disclosures provide a window into performance relative to the lofty projections made at IPO. Investors should track revenue growth, operating margins, customer churn, and any restatements or revisions. Discrepancies between pre-IPO forecasts and actual results can erode market trust.

Another dynamic to monitor is institutional accumulation. If large asset managers begin building positions or the company gains inclusion in indices like the S&P 500 or Nasdaq-100, it can drive sustained demand. These milestones often enhance visibility and improve liquidity, contributing to more stable pricing over time.

At the same time, investors must be wary of follow-on offerings. These occur when a newly public company issues additional shares to raise capital, potentially diluting existing shareholders. While not inherently negative, especially if funds are used for accretive growth, frequent or poorly timed secondary offerings may reflect weak capital discipline or cash flow challenges.

Effective post-IPO management from an investor's standpoint involves building a clear exit framework. Rather than reacting to short-term price swings, investors should assess whether valuation multiples remain aligned with earnings and growth trends. *Is the company progressing toward profitability? Are margins improving? Is management delivering on post-IPO guidance?*

Warning signs include slowing revenue momentum, missed earnings, insider stock dumping, or opaque financial disclosures. Companies that went public with the help of weak underwriters or filed S-1s hastily to capitalize on market sentiment should also be scrutinized. These are often signs that the IPO was a liquidity event, not a launchpad for sustainable value.

Ultimately, the post-IPO phase rewards investors who stay vigilant, skeptical, and focused on long-term fundamentals. The IPO may have opened the door, but what happens next determines whether a stock becomes a durable wealth builder or a short-lived hype cycle.

Robinhood's IPO and turbulent post-listing performance serve as a powerful example of the unique risks retail investors face after the public debut.

CASE STUDY: ROBINHOOD'S VOLATILE POST-IPO JOURNEY

Robinhood, the commission-free brokerage app, went public in July 2021 at $38 per share. The company's IPO was unconventional, as it reserved up to 35 percent of shares for retail investors, aiming to democratize access in line with its brand.

Initially, the IPO underwhelmed. Shares fell 8 percent on day one before surging 24 percent the next session. But within months, the stock experienced significant volatility, eventually dropping below $10 due to regulatory scrutiny, declining trading volumes, and concerns over revenue sustainability.

Post-IPO challenges included lock-up expirations, insider selling, and controversial decisions (such as halting trading in GameStop), which impacted brand trust. Institutional support faded, and Robinhood faced lawsuits, investigations, and increasing competition from Fidelity and Charles Schwab.

Investor Takeaway

Post-IPO management is just as critical as the IPO itself. Retail-access IPOs may appeal to individual investors, but exposure to volatile sentiment, weak fundamentals, or reputational risks can erode long-term value. Vigilant monitoring of earnings, insider activity, and regulatory risks is essential after the IPO bell rings.

CHAPTER 4

UNDERWRITER STABILIZATION AND THE GREENSHOE OPTION

Underwriters are more than middlemen in the IPO process; they act as gatekeepers and market makers. Their role goes beyond pricing the IPO and marketing the shares; they are responsible for ensuring a smooth public debut. This often includes short-term market interventions designed to reduce volatility and inspire investor confidence.

In the days following an IPO, newly listed stocks are particularly vulnerable to selling pressure. Early private investors may cash out, momentum traders may take profits, and short-sellers may test the market's strength. To counter this, underwriters may step in and purchase shares in the open market, a process known as price stabilization. While this doesn't guarantee a price floor, it can limit sharp declines and signal support, especially in high-profile offerings.

One of the most powerful tools underwriters use is the greenshoe option, a built-in mechanism that allows them to issue up to 15 percent more shares than initially planned. If demand is strong and the stock rises, the underwriter can purchase those extra shares at the IPO price to deliver them to investors, avoiding losses on oversold positions. If the stock falls, the underwriter can instead buy back shares on the open market at the lower price, effectively injecting demand and softening the decline. The greenshoe option allows underwriters to stabilize prices during the first thirty days of trading by either purchasing additional shares or selling short.

For investors, understanding the presence and use of a greenshoe option is critical. It's not just a technical mechanism; it's a signal of how much faith the underwriter has in the offering and how much short-term price volatility they are willing (or prepared) to manage. In many cases, stocks with fully exercised greenshoe options experience more orderly early trading, while those without stabilization support may face a rockier debut.

However, this support is temporary. Stabilization periods typically last no more than thirty days. Once the underwriter steps back, the stock is left to find its natural trading level based on fundamentals, sentiment, and market dynamics. If investor enthusiasm was driven more by marketing than by long-term value, prices can slip rapidly once artificial support is removed.

Investors should view underwriter behavior, how aggressively they support the IPO, whether the greenshoe is exercised, and how volume behaves post-listing as real-time signals of market health. While the underwriter's involvement may cushion early volatility, it is not a substitute for rigorous valuation analysis. Ultimately, the company's performance, not the underwriter's efforts, determines long-term returns.

SECONDARY OFFERINGS: THE IMPACT BEYOND THE IPO

An IPO is not the final stop on a company's capital-raising journey; it's often just the beginning. Many newly public companies return to the markets through secondary offerings, issuing additional shares to raise more funds. These events are common and not inherently negative. In fact, they can reflect smart strategic planning when timed right and deployed effectively.

Secondary offerings are typically used to fund expansion, make strategic acquisitions, retire debt, or seize the moment while the company's stock price is strong. When these proceeds are tied to high-ROI projects or balance sheet improvement, investors may view the offering positively over time. For example, funding a transformative acquisition or ramping up R&D in a high-growth segment could justify short-term dilution for long-term gains.

However, these offerings also carry risks, chief among them, dilution. Issuing new shares expands the share count, reducing the ownership percentage of existing shareholders. This can lead to immediate downward pressure on the stock price, particularly if the offering is perceived as opportunistic or poorly communicated. Investors must assess not just what capital is being raised for but why now and how often.

Repeated or poorly timed secondary offerings may signal that a company is struggling to generate cash internally. Worse, they can suggest that management is using favorable market conditions to raise money without a clear strategic plan. This behavior can erode investor trust, especially if there is a lack of transparency or if insiders are selling alongside the offering.

The timing of a secondary offering matters, too. Offerings conducted during a rally can appear opportunistic. Those that follow weak earnings or failed guidance may be seen as lifelines. Smart investors scrutinize the offering price relative to recent trading, review the underwriter's involvement, and examine whether insiders are participating (buying or selling).

Ultimately, secondary offerings are neither red flags nor green lights on their own; they are strategic moves that demand interpretation. Investors should ask: Will this capital be accretive to growth? Does it solve a problem or mask one? Is this a one-off decision or part of a pattern? Understanding these signals is essential for evaluating not just the offering itself but the long-term credibility of the management team and the sustainability of the business model.

MONITORING SHORT INTEREST AND MARKET SENTIMENT

In today's market environment, sentiment can move faster than fundamentals. Retail investors, empowered by commission-free trading platforms and online communities, can create sharp and sudden movements in stock prices. For IPO investors, understanding the mood of the market is no longer optional; it's a vital layer of post-listing analysis.

One of the most revealing tools in this context is short interest, the number of shares borrowed and sold in anticipation of buying them back at a lower price. Elevated short interest typically signals that a significant group of traders believes the stock is overvalued or likely to decline. In many cases, this skepticism is well-founded and precedes corrections. But when a heavily shorted stock delivers strong earnings or positive news, short sellers can get squeezed, triggering a sharp upward price spike as they rush to cover positions.

This phenomenon, known as a short squeeze, can create rare but explosive upside potential. For long investors, monitoring short interest provides a risk warning and a contrarian opportunity if the bearish consensus proves wrong. However, entering trades based solely on the possibility of a squeeze is speculative and should be approached with caution.

Beyond short interest, other sentiment signals can offer insight into market dynamics. A sudden spike in trading volume, especially following a quiet period, may indicate new institutional involvement or renewed retail enthusiasm. The initiation of analyst coverage, particularly from well-known firms, often brings added credibility and visibility to a stock. Even online chatter on platforms like Reddit, Twitter, or Stocktwits can foreshadow volatility, as retail-driven narratives gather momentum faster than traditional news cycles can respond.

That said, sentiment should never be mistaken for substance. These signals are transitory, prone to reversal, and often amplified by emotion rather than fact. While tracking sentiment can help investors anticipate market behavior, it should always be filtered through the lens of fundamentals, revenue growth, earnings performance, competitive advantage, and macroeconomic conditions. Sentiment may explain where the stock is trading today, but fundamentals still determine where it's likely to be tomorrow.

Savvy IPO investors recognize that market perception evolves quickly in the post-IPO window. By layering sentiment indicators onto rigorous analysis, they gain not only a pulse on crowd behavior but a deeper understanding of how conviction, momentum, and skepticism shape the stock's narrative in the public markets.

REVISITING YOUR INVESTMENT THESIS

An IPO often begins with excitement, promise, and polished storytelling. But once the company begins life as a public entity, the narrative meets reality. Quarterly earnings replace pitch decks, and analyst questions replace roadshow applause. For investors, this is the moment when your original thesis must evolve or be abandoned.

Post-IPO, companies are tested not only by markets but by time. The assumptions that drove your initial investment, around revenue growth, competitive advantage, and execution capability, must now be validated by actual performance. This is where discipline separates the speculative trader from the strategic investor.

Revenue growth remains the clearest signal of traction. Compare actual results against IPO projections. Is the company meeting its own forecasts? Is growth accelerating, plateauing, or slipping? Pay attention to year-over-year and quarter-over-quarter trends, as well as any changes in customer acquisition, churn, or product mix.

Competitive dynamics can also shift quickly. A disruptive IPO company may find its advantage eroded by a faster-moving rival, regulatory pressures, or macroeconomic headwinds. Staying informed about the company's positioning within its industry and how competitors are reacting can reveal whether its edge is durable or fading.

Management execution is often the most underappreciated factor. The same leadership team that dazzled during the roadshow may struggle under the burden of public market reporting, investor expectations, and operational scale. Watch for signs of strategic drift, missed milestones, or high executive turnover, all of which may suggest deeper issues.

Smart investors revisit their thesis regularly, not reactively after a price drop but proactively each quarter. Ask: Is the original story still intact? Has new information materially changed my outlook? If I didn't already own the stock, would I buy it today?

These reflections help sharpen conviction or justify exit. A strong thesis playing out as expected may call for holding or even increasing your position. A thesis that has deteriorated due to underperformance, market shifts, or management missteps may warrant a measured exit or a shift in strategy.

The key is to treat your IPO investment like a living decision, not a static bet. Revisiting your thesis ensures you're not anchored to past beliefs but are continually aligned with current realities and future opportunities.

THE INVESTOR'S IPO MINDSET

An IPO is not the finish line; it's the starting gate. Once a company goes public, the real work begins for the business and its investors. The post-IPO landscape introduces a new level of transparency, scrutiny, and volatility. Temporary price support from underwriters may ease early trading jitters, but once that stabilizing force disappears, stock performance becomes a pure reflection of fundamentals, sentiment, and execution.

In this environment, success depends on mindset. The investor's IPO mindset is not about chasing hype or predicting perfect timing; it's about building and following a disciplined, adaptive framework. IPO investing rewards those who can think in stages, analyze in context, and act with clarity amid noise.

This approach requires investors to be proactive and patient. It means tracking early underwriter activity, understanding when a secondary offering is strategic or dilutive, reading short interest as a sentiment signal rather than a headline, and revisiting your investment thesis with every new data point. It also means resisting the temptation to react emotionally to daily price swings fueled by retail momentum, media buzz, or social media chatter.

Discipline and data, not emotion and urgency, form the foundation of the IPO mindset. Investors must be willing to update their views as new information emerges while staying anchored to long-term goals. Strategic thinking, rigorous research, and a well-articulated exit or holding plan transform IPO investing from speculation into a repeatable strategy.

Ultimately, IPOs are high-stakes moments where optimism meets accountability. Some companies rise to the challenge. Others stumble. The investors best positioned to succeed are those who treat the IPO not as an event but as a process, one that demands attention, structure, and, above all, perspective.

FINAL TAKEAWAYS

IPO investing is not a gamble; it's a strategy. From pre-IPO selection to post-listing performance management, each phase of the journey demands a clear lens, a steady hand, and a commitment to evidence-based decision-making.

In the pre-IPO phase, the goal is access with insight. Investors must focus on companies with credible leadership, realistic valuations, and scalable business models. Assess the fundamentals, interrogate the narrative, and understand the risks of illiquidity and information asymmetry before capital is committed.

During the IPO execution window, timing is everything. Pay close attention to pricing signals, oversubscription data, and the reputation of underwriters. Institutional participation often sets the tone for initial performance. Retail investors must navigate allocation challenges and avoid the psychological traps of hype, FOMO, and herd behavior.

After the IPO, the real test begins. Monitor earnings reports, insider activity, and secondary offerings. Evaluate whether the company is living up to its promises and whether management is adapting to the scrutiny of the public markets. Be alert to dilution risks, sentiment shifts, and evolving market dynamics that may impact your thesis.

Across all stages, one principle holds: discipline drives outcomes. Investors who apply structured analysis, revisit their positions regularly, and make data-driven adjustments are far better equipped to navigate the volatility and opportunity that IPOs present.

IPO investing isn't about catching lightning in a bottle. It's about building a durable approach that balances conviction with flexibility and optimism with realism. With the right mindset, tools, and process, investors can turn these high-profile market moments into meaningful, long-term value.

CHAPTER 5

Evaluating IPO Prospects

IDENTIFYING WINNERS AND AVOIDING PITFALLS

Investing in an IPO is an exercise in evaluating potential while navigating limited publicly available data. Unlike established public companies with years of historical performance, IPOs operate under strict regulatory constraints that limit pre-listing disclosures. For investors, this creates a unique challenge: making high-stakes decisions with incomplete information, often under the pressure of media buzz and market speculation.

IPOs can be a gateway to explosive returns, but they can also be value traps wrapped in hype. The difference lies in how well an investor can interpret the fundamentals beneath the surface. These fundamentals, including revenue quality, margin strength, burn rate, market positioning, and leadership credibility, are the real indicators of long-term potential.

Yet, even seasoned investors can be lured by branding, valuation headlines, or herd behavior. This chapter provides a disciplined framework to cut through the noise, apply rigorous analysis, and assess IPOs with clarity. Hype fades, but execution endures. Understanding what really drives post-IPO success helps investors make informed decisions, manage risk, and avoid the common traps that have derailed even the most anticipated offerings.

FINANCIAL PERFORMANCE AND METRICS

Before an IPO, most companies haven't yet proven themselves in the public arena, and that makes financial analysis more difficult and more critical. Investors must look beyond surface-level numbers to uncover whether a business is truly built for long-term growth or simply engineered for a market debut.

When you invest in an IPO, you're often buying into potential, not performance. So, what separates viable growth from financial storytelling? It begins with revenue, not just *how much* but *how it's earned.*

Revenue Quality and Stability

Recurring revenue models, like subscriptions, provide greater predictability and reduce dependency on single transactions. Investors should determine whether a company's revenue is recurring or transactional and how diversified it is across products, services, and regions. Greater diversification often signals financial resilience.

Margins and Efficiency

Gross margin, the percentage of revenue remaining after production costs, is a clear indicator of pricing power and operational efficiency. Higher margins suggest a competitive advantage, while declining margins may signal rising costs or increased competition. Comparing these margins to industry peers helps investors evaluate strategic strength.

Operating Leverage and Cost Control

Companies that scale revenue without equally scaling operating expenses benefit from operating leverage, a key driver of profitability over time. Watch for decreasing Selling, General, and Administrative expenses (SG&A) as a percentage of revenue, as well as disciplined Research and Development (R&D) spending. High R&D isn't inherently bad; it can signal innovation, but it must be intentional and aligned with future growth.

Cash Flow and Burn Rate

The *burn rate* refers to the rate at which a company spends its available capital; essentially, how quickly it's "burning" through cash. A high burn rate is common in early-stage companies, but it must be matched with a clear path to profitability or access to additional capital. Negative free cash flow doesn't automatically disqualify a company, but it raises questions about capital efficiency and sustainability. Look for healthy liquidity ratios and evidence of strong expense management. Companies that frequently rely on secondary offerings to raise capital often dilute shareholder value and may signal operational instability.

Debt and Financial Leverage

Debt is not inherently bad; if used strategically, it can fund growth. But excessive leverage reduces flexibility and raises default risk during downturns. Examine debt-to-equity and interest coverage ratios. Ask: Is the company using debt to invest in the future or to cover for shortfalls in the present?

Working Capital Health

Key indicators such as Days Sales Outstanding (DSO), Days Payable Outstanding (DPO), and inventory turnover show how efficiently a company is managing cash in and out. High DSO can signal difficulty collecting revenue.

Meanwhile, consistent seasonality or cyclicality may affect cash flow, especially in sectors like retail, travel, or energy.

Use of Proceeds and Capital Planning
How a company plans to use its IPO proceeds says a lot about its priorities. Proceeds directed toward growth (like expansion or innovation) signal long-term strategy. Proceeds used to pay down debt or cover losses may raise concerns about financial health. Repeated capital raises without operational improvement are red flags.

Sector-Specific Context
Every industry has its own valuation logic. In tech and biotech, growth potential and intellectual property often outweigh immediate profitability. Investors must assess a company's financial performance relative to sector norms, not just general benchmarks.

In 2023, for example, the Rule of 40, a SaaS industry metric that combines revenue growth and profit margin, became the dominant valuation driver for SaaS companies in public markets, with revenue growth and Net Dollar Retention (NDR) a measure of how much recurring revenue grows or shrinks from existing customers tied for second.

Market Position and Differentiation
In the public markets, it is not enough to be promising; a company must be defensible. IPO investors are not just backing growth, they are betting on durability. The real question is: *Does this company have a moat?*

A competitive moat, built from brand strength, intellectual property, pricing power, or network effects, allows a company to fend off rivals and preserve margins even under pressure. Without this, even a fast-growing IPO can quickly lose altitude in the public markets.

Moats and Barriers to Entry

Investors should examine whether a company has real, enforceable barriers to entry. These may include proprietary technology, exclusive partnerships, regulatory approvals, or high capital requirements. Intellectual property (including patents, trade secrets, and trademarks) is a powerful shield. So is deep customer integration or long-term contracts. Without these protective features, even compelling business models may be easily copied or outpaced.

Market Share and Momentum

Market share tells a story: Is the company gaining ground, holding firm, or losing relevance? Leadership in a fast-growing market is more promising than a minor presence in a stagnant sector. However, size alone is not enough. Investors should analyze customer acquisition costs (CAC), churn rates, and customer lifetime value (CLV) to determine whether growth is sustainable. High CAC or heavy discounting may inflate short-term results while masking weak underlying economics.

Brand Strength and Ecosystem Power

A well-recognized brand can justify premium pricing and drive customer loyalty. Investors should look for indicators such as net promoter scores (NPS), customer sentiment, and brand awareness. Companies that operate within strong partner ecosystems through supplier exclusivity, product integrations, or platform partnerships are often better insulated from competitive pressure.

Scalability and Cost Structure

Some companies grow revenue without increasing profit, while others scale efficiently by leveraging automation, process discipline, and supply chain strength to expand operations. IPO investors should pay close attention to business models that scale intelligently rather than merely quickly. Economies of scale, platform efficiencies, and technology-enabled delivery models can turn early traction into long-term advantage.

Macroeconomic Tailwinds and Sector Positioning
External factors matter. Industries such as artificial intelligence, climate technology, and digital health benefit from strong tailwinds that include policy support, technological innovation, and evolving consumer behavior. These trends can enhance early performance, but they may also contribute to overvaluation. Investors must determine whether a company is leading the trend with a genuine advantage or simply following it to capitalize on short-term enthusiasm.

Differentiation in a Crowded Market
In saturated industries, differentiation is critical. Investors should look for unique value propositions, whether through novel products, superior service models, advanced data capabilities, or customer-focused innovation. A company that competes solely on price is unlikely to defend its margins after going public. The ability to evolve in response to disruption, or even anticipate it, is essential for long-term survival.

Regulatory Positioning and Strategic Strategy
Operating in highly regulated industries can serve as a strategic advantage, particularly when a company already holds key licenses or approvals. Regulatory compliance can limit new entrants. Additionally, investors should evaluate whether the company is a first mover, establishing a new category, or a fast follower that improves upon existing models. Both approaches can succeed, but each requires precision and timing.

Concentration Risk

Companies that rely heavily on a single region, product, or customer face significant exposure to disruption. Geographic and customer diversification signals greater stability. While international operations can broaden revenue streams, they also introduce additional risks such as currency fluctuations, regulatory complexity, and geopolitical uncertainty. A well-balanced revenue mix across customer segments and geographies reduces the potential for volatility.

The IPO Timing Trap

Some companies go public primarily to capitalize on sector enthusiasm rather than because they are ready for sustained public scrutiny. Investors should be cautious of IPOs in trending sectors such as artificial intelligence, electric vehicles, or biotechnology, particularly when the business fundamentals appear unproven. A strong opening day is not a guarantee of long-term performance. Competitive analysis, including whether a product or service can be easily replicated, should take precedence over market sentiment.

Ultimately, IPO investors must ask: *What would it take for a competitor to replace this company in three years?* If the answer is "not much," then the risk may be significantly higher than the prospectus suggests.

THE MANAGEMENT TEAM AND INSIDER COMMITMENTS

In IPO investing, leadership is not a soft metric; it is a critical form of risk. The management team you back on IPO day will be responsible for guiding the company through its most volatile period. Even the best business model can fail under poor execution, and investors must assess leadership with the same discipline they apply to financial analysis.

A management team with prior experience running a public company holds a significant advantage. Public markets demand a specialized skill set, including the ability to manage quarterly earnings expectations, regulatory compliance, investor relations, and media scrutiny. In contrast, inexperienced teams may struggle to adapt to these pressures, potentially damaging investor confidence and market stability. Investors should research past performance, especially how leadership navigated economic shifts or industry-specific headwinds.

A strong and independent board of directors plays a central role in ensuring effective governance and balanced decision-making. Investors should examine whether the board brings diverse experience across finance, legal, operations, and the relevant industry. The presence of respected advisors or former public company executives can signal maturity and readiness. A weak or founder-controlled board may raise concerns about accountability, especially in high-growth or founder-led companies.

CASE STUDY: UBER (2019): WHEN HYPE MEETS THE LOCK-UP CLIFF

Uber's IPO in May 2019 was one of the most anticipated tech listings in history. Backed by SoftBank and known for its global dominance in ridesharing, the company debuted at $45 per share, raising $8.1 billion. But despite the excitement, investors were wary. Uber had posted $2.9 billion in losses in the year prior to listing, and regulatory headwinds, including driver classification disputes, loomed large.

After an already underwhelming public debut, a critical inflection point came on November 6, 2019, when the 180-day lock-up period expired. Suddenly, 760 million *previously restricted shares—more than doubling the public float—flooded the market. The stock dropped 38.6 percent from its IPO price to $27.00, with an abnormal return of -4.1 percent on the day. Trading volume spiked 30 percent as early investors and employees rushed to offload their stakes. The mass selling signaled a lack of insider confidence and sent a clear message to the market.*

For investors, Uber's experience was a stark reminder that high insider selling, when combined with unproven profitability and weak governance controls, can magnify post-IPO risk. While Uber has since rebounded, reaching a $166 billion market cap by 2025, early public investors faced prolonged uncertainty and steep volatility.

Key Takeaway

Even the most recognizable companies can stumble without strong fundamentals. Lock-up expirations expose investor sentiment and management conviction, both of which matter more than hype.

Compensation Structures and Incentive Alignment

Compensation should be structured to reward long-term performance, not short-term stock movements. Look for equity-based compensation tied to clearly defined performance milestones, such as revenue growth, Earnings Before Interest, Taxes, Depreciation, and Amortization (EBITDA) margin expansion, or customer retention. When executive pay rises independently of company performance, it suggests poor governance and misaligned incentives.

Insider Behavior and Shareholder Trust

Insider ownership is a powerful signal. Executives who retain meaningful equity stakes have a strong personal incentive to build long-term value. However, investors should scrutinize insider selling patterns before and after the IPO. Heavy insider sales, particularly when combined with a dual-class share structure that limits shareholder influence, may indicate a lack of confidence or potential governance risks. A lock-up period, where insiders are restricted from selling shares immediately post-IPO, is often a positive sign of alignment with new investors.

Succession Planning and Leadership Continuity

Stability at the executive level is key during the transition to public markets. High turnover in the C-suite, especially near the IPO event, can be a red flag. Investors should review whether the company has a clear succession plan for critical roles and whether transitions have been communicated transparently. Leadership continuity can provide confidence during early-stage volatility.

Investor Relations and Market Communication

Public companies must master the art of investor engagement. Transparent earnings guidance, proactive communication during periods of uncertainty, and consistent strategic messaging help build investor trust. A strong investor relations (IR) function is not just about marketing; it is a vital feedback loop between leadership and the market. Investors should evaluate how clearly executives articulate goals and how effectively they respond to investor concerns.

CHAPTER 5

Regulatory Preparedness and Internal Controls

Going public comes with new responsibilities. Companies must meet SEC reporting standards, file regular disclosures, and manage internal controls with rigor. Leadership teams with prior public company experience are better positioned to avoid compliance missteps, accounting irregularities, or delayed filings. A well-prepared company should already have internal controls in place before the IPO, not build them after the fact.

Ethics, Culture, and Reputational Risk

Ethical leadership is not just a moral virtue; it is a business imperative. Companies with a history of ethical lapses, toxic workplace culture, or legal disputes may struggle to retain talent and attract investors. Conversely, companies that emphasize transparency, stakeholder engagement, and social responsibility often trade at a premium. Investors should look for companies with published ESG practices, whistleblower protections, and a public track record of responsible behavior.

Resilience and Strategic Foresight

Public markets reward companies that can adapt and execute. Investors should evaluate how the leadership team has responded to prior crises, such as supply chain disruptions, regulatory shifts, or competitive threats. Does the company have a defined risk management strategy? Has leadership demonstrated flexibility in strategy while maintaining discipline in execution? A resilient management team is often the deciding factor between a company that thrives post-IPO and one that stumbles.

Vision, Execution, and Market Readiness

Finally, investors should assess whether leadership is forward-thinking. Do executives have a clear vision for market expansion, product evolution, and competitive positioning? Companies led by visionaries with a track record of making bold but disciplined strategic moves tend to outperform over time. An IPO should be a launchpad for growth, not an endpoint. Leadership is what determines whether that launch is successful.

Operational Readiness and Scalability

Investors often focus on revenue projections, but without a scalable foundation, growth can quickly become a liability. At IPO, a company must prove it can grow without collapsing under the weight of its own expansion. Operational readiness is not only about capacity; it is about resilience, discipline, and foresight.

Scalability starts with infrastructure. Investors should assess whether the company's supply chain, production capacity, and logistics are equipped to handle rising demand. A weak operational backbone can result in fulfillment delays, quality issues, and margin erosion. The use of third-party vendors, inventory management practices, and vendor concentration risk should all be evaluated to identify potential bottlenecks.

Technology also plays a central role in scalability. Companies that deploy automation and cloud-based systems are better positioned to manage complexity, reduce costs, and maintain service quality. Investors should examine the company's IT systems, software architecture, and cybersecurity protocols. A data breach, system outage, or legacy tech platform can create operational chaos and reputational damage. Technology should not just support growth; it should *enable* it.

Compliance readiness is another vital signal of a company's maturity. Public companies face elevated regulatory expectations, and weak governance frameworks often result in costly delays, restatements, or fines. Investors should verify that the company has internal audit functions, financial reporting controls, and cross-functional compliance teams in place before going public. Last-minute compliance catch-up is a warning sign of deeper structural risk.

People as a Scaling Engine

Growth requires people, not just systems. Human capital management should be treated as a frontline IPO metric. Investors should evaluate whether the company can recruit, retain, and develop talent at scale. This includes succession planning, training frameworks, employee engagement, and competitive compensation practices. Startups often rely on a few key individuals; public companies need teams that can scale performance consistently.

Leadership bench strength is equally critical. A company that scales too fast without investing in managerial depth may encounter cultural breakdowns, operational blind spots, or governance drift. Investors should ask: Who will lead the next stage of growth? Is there a plan if a founder or key executive exits?

RIVIAN (2021): A TEXTBOOK CASE OF OVERPROMISED, UNDER-DELIVERED

Electric vehicle startup Rivian exploded onto the public markets in November 2021 with one of the biggest U.S. IPOs since 2014. Priced at $78 per share, the stock soared to nearly $180 within days, briefly valuing the pre-revenue *company at over $120 billion. Backed by Amazon and Ford, Rivian had every signal of a "next big thing."*

But as the months unfolded, cracks began to show. By the end of 2022, Rivian had delivered just over 7,300 vehicles—far short of its 25,000 goal. Losses widened to $1.7 billion in Q3 alone, and ongoing production delays eroded investor confidence. By early 2025, the stock hovered around $15, a collapse of over 85 percent from its peak. However, it should also be noted that Rivian's revenue grew significantly during this time, from $55 million in 2021 to over $5 billion by 2024.

Rivian's operational readiness simply did not match the scale of investor expectations. The company struggled with manufacturing ramp-up, supply chain logistics, and competitive pressures from Tesla and legacy automakers. The result was a rapid deflation of valuation, and a cautionary tale for investors.

Key Takeaway

Momentum can drive a strong debut, but it cannot compensate for lack of operational execution. For IPO investors, scalability is not a future goal; it is a day-one requirement.

CUSTOMER AND REVENUE CONCENTRATION

Scalability also depends on customer base diversification. Companies that rely on a single client, channel, or region may grow quickly but remain exposed to outsized risk. Investors should examine how revenue is distributed across geographies and customer segments. Broader diversification enhances resilience and helps smooth performance during market shifts.

RISK MANAGEMENT AND ESG INTEGRATION

Operational readiness is not just about growth; it is about control. Public companies face risks on multiple fronts, from shareholder activism to supply chain disruption. Investors should look for companies with active risk registers, contingency planning, and executive-led crisis response systems.

Increasingly, institutional investors expect companies to integrate Environmental, Social, and Governance (ESG) principles into their operations. ESG is no longer a side consideration; it reflects a company's long-term thinking and stakeholder awareness. Sustainability goals, ethical supply chains, and community engagement can reduce reputational risk and enhance brand value. Companies that bake ESG into their operational DNA are often rewarded with stronger investor confidence and greater access to long-term capital.

In short, operational readiness signals whether a company is built to grow or poised to falter under pressure. Investors must ask not only whether the company can scale but whether it can scale *well*.

FINAL TAKEAWAYS

Investing in IPOs is not about chasing headlines or hoping to ride the next unicorn wave. It is about disciplined evaluation, informed decision-making, and strategic timing. While media buzz can fuel excitement, smart investors resist the noise and stay grounded in the fundamentals.

The strongest IPO opportunities emerge when a company demonstrates sustainable revenue growth, experienced and accountable leadership, strong operational readiness, and a defensible market position. These are the markers of long-term potential, not just short-term price spikes.

A structured evaluation process allows investors to filter through hype, identify red flags early, and focus on companies that are built to endure. Reviewing financial metrics, management alignment, competitive advantages, and readiness to scale can help protect capital and improve returns over time.

Ultimately, IPO investing rewards those who ask the right questions, demand transparency, and think long-term. A commitment to due diligence and investor discipline will always outperform impulsive speculation. The market will reward insight, not instinct.

CHAPTER 6

Understanding the IPO Prospectus Decoding the Investment Narrative

Investing in IPOs can be fraught with risk. While the promise of rapid growth attracts many, historical data reveals a sobering reality: a significant percentage of IPOs underperform the broader market within their first year of trading. The exact percentage can vary depending on the time period and market conditions. Studies often cite figures in the range of 50–60 percent, but this requires attribution to specific research or data sources for accuracy. For example, a study by Ritter (University of Florida) often highlights underperformance trends in IPOs. This highlights the critical importance of understanding the IPO prospectus, an investor's key to navigating the investment narrative and separating promising investments from those more likely to underperform.

At its core, the IPO prospectus is a company's formal pitch to investors, blending storytelling with financial and regulatory disclosure. It serves as a sales document and a risk disclosure, requiring careful scrutiny to discern the reality behind a company's ambitions. This chapter outlines the purpose, accessibility, and key components of an IPO prospectus, enabling investors to develop a critical eye for evaluating new public offerings.

THE PURPOSE OF THE IPO PROSPECTUS

An IPO prospectus (S-1 or F-1) is more than a regulatory hoop to jump through; it is the company's sales pitch, risk disclosure document, and financial report card all rolled into one. It is a carefully crafted narrative designed to convince investors that the company deserves their capital. However, every story has a spin.

The prospectus serves as a legally mandated disclosure document, ensuring compliance with securities laws and protecting both investors and the issuing company. By detailing material facts, financial data, and risk factors, it provides transparency that allows potential shareholders to make informed decisions. Beyond its legal function, the prospectus plays a crucial role in shaping investor confidence and market perception. A well-structured and thorough prospectus signals credibility, influencing both demand for shares and the IPO's pricing.

The prospectus outlines the company's business model, strategy, and financial condition. This allows investors to analyze the firm in the context of its industry, comparing key performance metrics against competitors. The depth of financial and operational information facilitates a thorough evaluation, making it possible to assess whether the company is positioned for sustainable growth. Equally important is the section detailing how the IPO proceeds will be used. Investors examine whether the capital raised will drive meaningful expansion, fund research and development, reduce debt, or support acquisitions, all of which provide insight into the company's priorities and long-term vision.

The prospectus also sheds light on corporate governance and leadership. The experience and track record of the management team are critical factors in an investment decision, as strong leadership increases the likelihood of effective execution. Investors scrutinize this section to determine whether seasoned executives with a history of delivering results are guiding the company. Furthermore, the presence of respected underwriters lends additional credibility, as these institutions conduct their own due diligence before backing an IPO. Institutional investors pay close attention to these endorsements, often using them as indicators of a company's market potential.

While the prospectus may include forward-looking statements about projected earnings and growth, investors must remember that these are based on assumptions, not guarantees. Companies often present pro forma figures or adjusted earnings that paint a more favorable financial picture. Pro forma figures and adjusted earnings are standard in IPO prospectuses to provide a clearer picture of financial performance by excluding one-time or non-recurring items. However, these adjustments must comply with regulatory guidelines, such as those set by the SEC, and are disclosed transparently in the prospectus. Experienced investors understand the importance of scrutinizing footnotes and the fine print, where key accounting assumptions are often buried. The prospectus may be thorough, but its language is carefully curated, and areas where the phrasing is vague or evasive often hint at the biggest red flags.

Beyond the IPO itself, the level of transparency in the prospectus can influence a company's post-listing performance. Companies that set clear, realistic expectations tend to perform better in public markets, while those that overpromise often face volatility once their financials come under greater scrutiny. Reading a prospectus is not just about understanding what is presented; it is about identifying what is missing. Investors should continually ask: What information is not being disclosed?

NAVIGATING THE EDGAR DATABASE

The prospectus is publicly available through the SEC's EDGAR database (www.sec.gov/edgar), a powerful resource that provides direct access to IPO filings and other regulatory documents. While EDGAR may initially appear overwhelming, learning to navigate it effectively can save time and help investors locate the right filings with ease.

On the main search page, entering a company's full name or its unique Central Index Key (CIK) retrieves all related filings. Since IPO prospectuses are classified under "S-1" or "F-1" forms, filtering by form type quickly narrows the results to the most relevant documents. The "S-1" form applies to U.S.-based companies, while "F-1" forms are for foreign entities listing on U.S. exchanges. Investors should also be aware of amendments (e.g., S-1/A), which indicate updates to the initial filing. The filing date is equally important, as companies often submit multiple amendments throughout the IPO process. Ensuring that the latest available version is reviewed, typically marked as the final or effective prospectus, is critical in obtaining the most accurate and complete information.

For those requiring a more refined search, EDGAR's advanced tools allow filtering by specific date ranges, form types, or filing categories. This is particularly useful when comparing multiple IPOs within a certain period or analyzing historical trends. Although EDGAR presents raw filings in their official legal format, a structured approach to searching can help investors bypass unnecessary clutter and focus on the data that matters most. With practice, what initially seems like a complex system becomes an invaluable tool for conducting due diligence and uncovering insights that might otherwise go unnoticed.

CHAPTER 6

BUSINESS OVERVIEW

The Business Overview section serves as the company's narrative, outlining its mission, core products or services, target market, and competitive positioning. This section is designed to present a compelling case for investment, making it essential to assess whether the business has a clear and differentiated value proposition.

Beyond the surface-level description, it is important to identify concrete details that validate the company's claims. A thorough review involves analyzing whether the company breaks down its revenue, margins, and growth potential by business line or segment. Companies with multiple product categories or service offerings should disclose the relative contribution of each, allowing for evaluation of which areas drive profitability and where potential risks may lie. The presence of detailed financial data signals transparency, whereas vague or generalized statements may indicate an attempt to obscure underperforming segments.

A well-articulated roadmap for growth is another critical element of this section. A realistic strategy for expansion, such as entering new geographic markets, launching additional product lines, or forming strategic partnerships, should be supported by credible execution plans. Comparing management's stated goals with industry benchmarks and historical performance can provide a valuable perspective on whether the company's ambitions are grounded in reality.

Since every company positioning itself for an IPO aims to present an attractive growth story, a degree of skepticism is warranted. The Business Overview should be evaluated not only for its content but also for any notable omissions. If details on customer retention, market share, or competitive risks are absent, these gaps may indicate potential concerns. A well-structured Business Overview balances ambition with substance, offering a clear picture of the company's market position and future trajectory.

RISK FACTORS

The Risk Factors section is one of the most critical parts of the prospectus, providing insight into the challenges and uncertainties that could impact the company's future performance. While every IPO filing includes this section as a regulatory requirement, the most informative disclosures distinguish between generic risks and those that are material and company-specific.

Common red flags include:

- Overly generic language
- Absence of mitigation strategies
- Misalignment between stated risks and the broader company narrative

Investors should pay close attention to whether the risks outlined are substantive or merely boilerplate disclaimers. Some companies rely on broad language to cover standard uncertainties without offering meaningful insight into their unique exposure. The more detailed and tailored the risk disclosure, the more transparent the company is likely to be.

Equally important is the inclusion of credible plans for mitigating the identified risks. If a significant challenge is highlighted, such as reliance on a single supplier, exposure to geopolitical instability, or pending litigation, it is important that a corresponding contingency plan is discussed. A prospectus that lists risks without outlining strategic responses may signal weak leadership or a lack of preparedness. In contrast, companies that acknowledge challenges while demonstrating proactive risk management inspire greater investor confidence.

This section should not be read in isolation but considered alongside other disclosures. For example, if the Business Overview emphasizes aggressive expansion while the Risk Factors cite economic uncertainty without clarifying how such risks will be managed, there may be a disconnect in the company's strategy. Investors benefit from applying a critical lens to determine whether leadership is equipped to navigate the potential threats outlined.

USE OF PROCEEDS

The Use of Proceeds section outlines how the company intends to allocate the capital raised from the IPO, offering valuable insight into its strategic priorities and financial health. A well-defined breakdown of fund allocation demonstrates a clear vision for growth, whereas vague or overly broad descriptions may suggest a lack of direction. Investors should pay close attention to whether the company provides specific details about how the proceeds will be deployed, as this can be a strong indicator of future performance and management's ability to execute its plans effectively.

Transparent allocation builds investor trust and signals management's strategic clarity. A company that directs IPO proceeds toward research and development, product expansion, or scaling into new markets signals a forward-looking approach aimed at long-term value creation. Strategic investments in technology, infrastructure, or acquisitions may also suggest an intent to strengthen competitive positioning. On the other hand, a heavy allocation toward debt repayment may indicate financial strain or poor historical cash flow management.

While paying down debt is not inherently negative, it is important to evaluate whether the debt was incurred to fund expansion or if it reflects past financial mismanagement. Broad terms such as "general corporate purposes" are common but may raise questions if left unexplained. Some flexibility in fund usage is reasonable, but a lack of transparency can indicate that management has not fully articulated its capital deployment strategy.

Comparing the Use of Proceeds section with the company's financial statements and business strategy helps investors determine whether the capital is being used to drive sustainable growth or simply to stabilize existing operations. Ultimately, this section should align with the company's stated objectives in the Business Overview and Risk Factors sections. Any inconsistencies between stated goals and capital allocation plans may suggest a need for deeper scrutiny.

MANAGEMENT'S DISCUSSION AND ANALYSIS (MD&A)

The Management's Discussion and Analysis (MD&A) section provides a window into how company leadership interprets past performance and envisions future growth. More than just a recap of financial results, this section enables investors to assess the credibility and strategic thinking of the management team. A strong MD&A provides data-driven insights, explaining not only what occurred but why, while also outlining how leadership plans to navigate future challenges and opportunities.

A well-constructed MD&A goes beyond optimistic projections by including concrete metrics and logical rationale for anticipated growth. For example, if management expects revenue to increase due to market expansion or product innovation, those expectations should be backed by supporting data, such as historical performance trends, customer demand, or competitive positioning.

An honest discussion of risks, such as supply chain constraints, regulatory pressures, or shifting market dynamics, demonstrates a realistic and accountable leadership approach. Companies that acknowledge potential headwinds while outlining strategic responses are more likely to inspire confidence than those that gloss over difficulties. Cross-checking the MD&A with financial statements is essential for verifying the narrative. If strong revenue growth is emphasized while margins are declining, such inconsistencies may indicate hidden vulnerabilities.

Additionally, if a company highlights plans to enter new markets, the Use of Proceeds section should support these claims with specific allocations toward expansion efforts. The MD&A serves as a test of management's transparency, analytical depth, and ability to execute. Companies that present well-articulated, data-backed analysis signal strong governance and a disciplined approach to growth. Conversely, generic optimism without supporting evidence may warrant further investigation.

FINANCIAL STATEMENTS

The Financial Statements section provides a quantitative snapshot of a company's financial health, offering a foundation for evaluating investment potential. While a deep accounting background is not necessary, understanding key financial trends and ratios is essential for making informed decisions. The financial data should either confirm or challenge the broader investment narrative presented throughout the prospectus.

Revenue growth is often one of the most telling indicators of market traction. A consistent upward trend suggests increasing demand, while stagnant or declining revenue raises questions about competitiveness, market saturation, or execution issues. However, revenue alone is not sufficient. Analyzing gross and operating margins offers deeper insight into the company's cost control and operational efficiency.

Cash flow from operations is a vital measure of financial sustainability. Positive cash flow suggests the company can fund its activities without relying excessively on outside capital. A business that consistently burns cash may depend heavily on IPO proceeds or debt, raising concerns about its long-term viability. Comparing trends in net income and cash flow can help reveal whether reported earnings are backed by actual liquidity.

Investors should also look for alignment between financial statements and other sections of the prospectus. For instance, if the company emphasizes investment in R&D or international expansion, past expenditures and capital allocations should reflect that strategy. Numbers can be framed in persuasive ways, so it is important to approach this section with a critical mindset. A company showing healthy growth, margins, and cash flow is better positioned for success, whereas financial inconsistencies may signal risks.

CASE STUDY: FACEBOOK – WHEN NARRATIVE OUTPACES EXECUTION

On May 18, 2012, Facebook made its long-awaited public debut, raising $16 billion in its initial public offering—$18.4 billion when including overallotments, making it one of the largest IPOs in U.S. history at the time. More than a financial milestone, the event marked the arrival of social media as a dominant force in the capital markets. Yet, despite the fanfare, Facebook's IPO offers a critical lesson in how investor expectations, shaped by the prospectus, must be grounded in executional clarity and financial discipline.

Business Overview

Facebook's prospectus centered around its mission to "make the world more open and connected," positioning its platform as a transformative force in global communication. The company emphasized its then-massive user base—over 900 million monthly active users—and its leading role in reshaping digital engagement. While the prospectus presented a compelling narrative of dominance and growth, it offered limited detail on revenue sources, particularly in mobile, an area where Facebook was already encountering monetization challenges. This omission illustrated how even dominant players may leave strategic blind spots unaddressed.

Risk Factors

Facebook's filing disclosed several meaningful risks:

- *Heavy reliance on advertising, which accounted for over 85 percent of revenue*
- *Lagging mobile monetization, despite growing mobile user engagement*
- *Privacy and regulatory concerns, especially around user data handling*

Although these disclosures signaled transparency, the accompanying mitigation strategies lacked clarity, highlighting operational vulnerabilities insufficiently addressed elsewhere in the filing.

Use of Proceeds

The company stated that proceeds would be used for "general corporate purposes," including working capital and potential acquisitions. While common, such phrasing can reduce transparency. In this case, the lack of specificity raised concerns about Facebook's plans to directly support its mobile transition or broader innovation strategy.

Management's Discussion and Analysis (MD&A)

The MD&A section underscored Facebook's explosive user and revenue growth. However, many observers criticized its tone as overly optimistic. Although the company referenced opportunities in mobile advertising, it lacked a clear roadmap for monetization. This disconnect between strategic ambitions and execution details proved to be a cautionary signal.

Financial Statements

Facebook's financials demonstrated strong top-line growth but also revealed declining margins, due largely to increased investments in infrastructure and platform development. This trade-off raised questions about scalability, particularly since monetization lagged behind user engagement.

Post-IPO Performance

Despite high investor interest, Facebook's stock price declined from its IPO price of $38 to under $20 within a few months. Contributing factors included:

- *Delays in adapting to mobile advertising*
- *Concerns over valuation*
- *Technical issues during trading on the Nasdaq*

However, Facebook ultimately executed a successful pivot to mobile, developing scalable, data-driven ad solutions. Within a few years, mobile advertising had become its core growth engine, reaffirming the company's long-term potential.

Investor Takeaways

- *A compelling mission is not a substitute for a clear execution strategy.*

- *General fund allocation language may reduce investor confidence.*
- *Identified risks must be paired with credible mitigation strategies.*
- *IPO valuation should align with near-term business readiness.*

Facebook's IPO illustrates both the power and limitations of the prospectus as an investment narrative. For investors, the lesson is clear: Understanding a prospectus requires reading between the lines, questioning omissions, and ensuring that storytelling aligns with strategic substance.

UNDERWRITING AND SHARE STRUCTURE

The Underwriting and Share Structure section provides insight into the mechanics of the IPO, revealing who is bringing the company public, how shares are allocated, and the potential impact on long-term shareholder value. The quality of underwriters often reflects market confidence, as top-tier investment banks tend to attract more institutional interest. These underwriters also help shape investor perception and stabilize early trading through marketing and pricing strategies.

Lock-up periods, typically ranging from 90 to 180 days, determine when insiders and early investors can sell shares. Some IPOs use staggered schedules, releasing shares at different intervals. A large influx of insider sales following a lock-up expiration can depress stock prices, especially if investor confidence is already fragile.

Share class structure is equally important. Dual-class structures common in the tech sector give insiders outsized voting rights while limiting public shareholder influence. While this can preserve a company's vision and leadership continuity, it can also reduce accountability to public investors.

Free float: the percentage of shares available for public trading, affects stock liquidity and volatility. A limited float can lead to price swings and reduced trading flexibility. It is important to assess how much of the company remains in pre-IPO hands and whether those holdings may be sold post-lock-up.

Dilution is another consideration. While raising capital is necessary, excessive issuance of new shares can reduce the ownership percentage and value of existing shareholders. Reviewing past funding rounds and the company's track record of capital allocation can help forecast whether further dilution is likely.

FINAL TAKEAWAYS

Scrutinizing the fine print of an IPO prospectus is essential. While the document is designed to present the company in the best possible light, a careful reader can uncover discrepancies, gaps, and signals of either discipline or risk. Assessing how a company allocates proceeds, discloses risks, and aligns its strategy with its financials helps investors identify IPOs with genuine long-term potential. A prospectus is not just a pitch; it is a blueprint for critical analysis.

CHAPTER 7

IPO Success vs. Failure

NAVIGATING THE IPO LANDSCAPE: KEY SUCCESS FACTORS

Every year, hundreds of companies go public, yet nearly half underperform the market within three years. What differentiates the winners from the laggards is execution. Successful IPOs are not just about ringing the bell; they require building sustainable value in the public markets. The strongest IPOs share a set of defining characteristics.

A significant market opportunity plays a critical role in attracting investor interest, particularly in high-growth sectors such as life sciences, fintech, and consumer technology. Industry leadership and market disruption further distinguish strong IPOs, as category leaders introducing game-changing solutions often see robust performance. Early access to emerging trends, such as AI, renewable energy, and cybersecurity, can generate strong demand.

Companies that succeed post-IPO are those with a clear path to profitability, even if they are not profitable at the time of listing. Investors are increasingly prioritizing financial discipline, predictable revenue streams, and strong margins over rapid, unprofitable expansion. A well-structured balance sheet, effective cost management, and a history of revenue growth demonstrate long-term viability and instill confidence in public market investors.

Beyond market opportunity and industry leadership, governance plays a crucial role in an IPO's success. Companies with strong governance structures, including a well-composed and independent board, transparent financial reporting, and shareholder-friendly policies, are more likely to build trust with institutional investors. A leadership team with a proven track record of executing growth strategies, managing public company responsibilities, and engaging with shareholders meaningfully can significantly impact post-IPO performance.

Institutional investor participation in an IPO often serves as a validation of the company's potential. When respected institutional investors and underwriters back an IPO, it signals confidence in the company's fundamentals. Strong pre-IPO investor demand can lead to oversubscription, often translating into post-listing stability and price appreciation. Companies that strategically cultivate long-term institutional investors rather than short-term speculative traders tend to have more sustained performance.

Companies that scale efficiently while maintaining operational discipline tend to outperform in the public markets. Scalable business models that leverage automation, global expansion, or platform-based solutions offer higher potential for exponential growth. Furthermore, businesses with strong competitive moats, such as proprietary technology, brand strength, or regulatory advantages, are better positioned to sustain their market leadership and fend off competition.

The timing of an IPO plays a significant role in its success. Companies that go public during bullish market conditions with strong investor appetite for growth tend to perform better initially. Conversely, those launching during periods of market uncertainty or economic downturns may struggle to maintain valuation post-listing. Understanding macroeconomic factors, interest rate environments, and overall risk sentiment is crucial in determining IPO timing.

An IPO is not the final destination but the beginning of a company's journey in the public markets. The best-performing IPOs maintain strong investor relations post-listing, clearly articulating their strategic vision, delivering on growth promises, and managing market expectations. Companies that actively engage with analysts, provide transparent guidance, and maintain consistent earnings growth tend to build a loyal investor base, reducing volatility and enhancing long-term shareholder value.

THE WEWORK IPO COLLAPSE: OVERVALUATION AND MISMANAGEMENT

The dramatic failure of WeWork's attempted IPO in 2019 stands as one of the most instructive cautionary tales in public market history. Once valued at $47 billion, the company's downfall was not merely a result of market forces; it was a direct consequence of overvaluation, poor governance, and a fundamentally flawed business model.

At the heart of WeWork's collapse was a culture of excessive hype, masking deep financial instability. Marketed as a revolutionary tech company disrupting office space, WeWork's business model involved leasing long-term office spaces and subleasing them on short-term agreements, which created a fundamental mismatch between revenue and costs. This mismatch contributed significantly to its financial instability.

Burning through billions annually without a clear path to profitability, the company lacked the financial discipline necessary for long-term success. Compounding these issues were CEO Adam Neumann's governance issues, which included self-dealing transactions (e.g., leasing properties he owned back to WeWork) and extravagant spending on personal luxuries like private jets.

Institutional investors and analysts, who had been bullish on high-growth startups, quickly distanced themselves from WeWork when they scrutinized its financials. The company's S-1 filing exposed unsustainable losses, a vague path to profitability, and governance red flags that made it a risky bet. The debacle highlighted the critical role of rigorous due diligence in IPO investing, reinforcing that even the most hyped companies must withstand financial scrutiny before entering the public markets.

The WeWork IPO was initially expected to be one of the largest of the year, but the company's valuation plummeted from $47 billion to as low as $10 billion in a matter of weeks. This abrupt decline not only burned early investors but also served as a warning for the broader market, cooling investor enthusiasm for unprofitable tech-driven startups. The ripple effect was seen in how SoftBank, the company's largest backer, was forced to write down billions, and it led to increased skepticism toward similar high-growth, high-burn-rate business models.

Neumann's unchecked authority, enabled by WeWork's dual-class share structure, allowed him to retain disproportionate control, making critical decisions without sufficient oversight. Investors learned a vital lesson: strong corporate governance and balanced leadership are non-negotiable in a public company. The absence of independent checks and balances creates excessive risk, as seen in Neumann's self-dealing transactions and erratic spending. This failure underscored why investors must evaluate a company's governance structure as closely as its financials.

The timing of WeWork's failed IPO also played a role in its downfall. In 2019, public market investors had become increasingly wary of high-profile, money-losing IPOs following disappointing debuts from companies like Uber and Lyft. This changing sentiment amplified scrutiny of WeWork's fundamentals, demonstrating the importance of market conditions in determining the success of an IPO. The lesson for investors is that even well-backed companies can falter if the timing and broader economic environment do not align.

WeWork's collapse reinforced the need for IPO investors to focus on sustainable business models, not just branding and market positioning. While vision and scale are important, they must be supported by solid financials, clear corporate governance, and a path to profitability.

Investors must ask tough questions: *Is the valuation justified? Is leadership trustworthy? Does the business have a defensible moat and a realistic growth strategy?* The WeWork case remains a stark reminder that the public markets reward discipline and punish excess.

When WeWork's financials were exposed, institutional investors recoiled. The IPO was swiftly pulled, its valuation plummeted, and the company narrowly avoided bankruptcy, salvaged only by a last-ditch bailout from SoftBank.

The WeWork saga underscores a crucial lesson: public markets demand transparency, accountability, and a sustainable business model. Companies built on overhyped valuations and weak governance structures cannot withstand investor scrutiny. Conversely, those prioritizing strong fundamentals, meticulous planning, and strategic market timing position themselves for IPO success.

THE THREE MAJOR PITFALLS OF THE WEWORK IPO

One of the key factors that led to WeWork's failure was the reliance on hype over fundamentals. Despite branding itself as a cutting-edge tech firm, WeWork was a real estate business with an unsustainable burn rate. When the numbers came to light, the illusion collapsed. Weak governance and oversight further exacerbated the situation. Neumann's unchecked control, reckless expenditures, and questionable self-dealing transactions signaled governance failures that shook investor confidence. Additionally, the company's misaligned business model made it impossible to justify its valuation. Over-reliance on intangible concepts like "community" and "culture" distracts from the harsh financial reality.

WeWork's excessive cash burn has become one of the most glaring red flags for investors. The company was locked in long-term lease commitments while offering flexible, short-term rental agreements to clients; a fundamental mismatch that exposed it to high financial risk. With annual losses surpassing $2 billion and no clear path to break even, WeWork's financial model was built on unsustainable growth rather than profitability. This was further exacerbated by the company's reliance on continuous capital infusions from private investors rather than demonstrating operational efficiency or positive unit economics.

The discrepancy between WeWork's private valuation and public market reality was stark. While venture capitalists poured billions into the company, focusing on topline growth, public investors demanded profitability, governance, and accountability, three areas where WeWork fell short. When the IPO filing laid bare its unprofitable business model, investors balked, leading to a sharp valuation decline from $47 billion to under $10 billion almost overnight. This dramatic re-rating demonstrated how public markets are fundamentally different from private ones, rewarding financial discipline over unchecked expansion.

Adam Neumann's charismatic leadership and grandiose vision were instrumental in attracting investor capital, but without proper oversight, they became liabilities. His unchecked authority led to a series of questionable financial decisions, including leasing properties he owned back to WeWork and personally cashing out nearly $700 million before the IPO. The absence of a strong board, coupled with a dual-class share structure that gave him disproportionate control, amplified the risks. Public investors viewed this as a serious governance failure, reinforcing the importance of independent oversight in any IPO-bound company.

An IPO cannot serve as a Band-Aid for structural weaknesses. Sustainable success in public markets requires strong corporate governance, a viable business strategy, and a valuation rooted in financial reality.

The WeWork case reinforced a crucial lesson for investors: brand narrative and aggressive expansion are not substitutes for a sound business model. Companies entering the public markets must demonstrate clear financial discipline, sustainable revenue streams, and governance structures that align leadership with shareholder interests. WeWork's inability to meet these criteria resulted in a failed IPO that served as a wake-up call for venture-backed companies seeking to go public without a clear path to profitability.

THE DIFFERENCE BETWEEN LASTING SUCCESS AND FADING HYPE

A well-prepared IPO is not just a capital-raising event; it is a company's first major test in the public markets. The transition from private to public status places an organization under a microscope, where financial discipline, strategic execution, and leadership credibility are constantly scrutinized. Companies that go public prematurely, without a clear operational roadmap and governance structure, risk becoming cautionary tales rather than success stories.

Public investors are not venture capitalists; they demand financial sustainability, transparency, and a clear growth trajectory. The most successful IPOs are those that tell a compelling, data-driven story, one rooted in business fundamentals rather than flashy marketing and aggressive valuation projections. Institutional investors, in particular, look for companies with disciplined financial management, a differentiated market position, and a leadership team capable of navigating public market pressures.

Timing also plays a crucial role. Even strong companies can struggle if they enter the public markets at the wrong time amid economic downturns, unfavorable investor sentiment, or a cooling IPO market. The ability to read market conditions and adjust accordingly is often the difference between a thriving public company and one that loses momentum shortly after listing.

Companies must recognize that an IPO is not the finish line but the starting point of an entirely new phase of corporate existence. The shift from private ownership to public accountability requires a mindset change, and quarterly earnings reports, regulatory scrutiny, and shareholder expectations all become integral to the company's daily operations. Those who embrace this shift with transparency, strategic foresight, and a commitment to long-term value creation will position themselves for sustained success.

WHAT LASTING SUCCESS LOOKS LIKE ON PAPER

From an investor's lens, lasting IPO success can often be identified by metrics like:

- Consistent revenue growth above 25–30 percent post-IPO

- Positive or improving free cash flow within 12–24 months
- Retention metrics such as Net Dollar Retention (NDR) > 110 percent
- Rule of 40 compliance (growth + profit margin > 40) in SaaS/tech IPOs
- Insider alignment, evidenced by significant equity ownership and minimal selling post-lockup

These indicators reflect strong execution, capital discipline, and alignment with shareholder interests.

HOW TO SPOT FADING HYPE

Investors should be cautious of companies with:

- Declining margins even as revenue increases
- Aggressive use of adjusted metrics with limited GAAP transparency
- Heavy reliance on vague KPIs (e.g., "engagement," "eyeballs") over revenue or cash flow
- CEO overreach, such as dual-class shares or limited board independence
- Poor post-IPO communications, like missed guidance or weak investor relations

These often signal a company not yet ready for the rigor of public markets.

CROWDSTRIKE'S SUCCESSFUL IPO

CrowdStrike exemplifies the power of a strong market opportunity driving IPO success. The cybersecurity firm went public on June 12, 2019, pricing shares at $34, above the expected range. Its leadership position in cybersecurity, cutting-edge technology, and strong financial growth fueled overwhelming investor demand.

CrowdStrike's IPO success was not just about entering a high-growth market; it was a case study in precise execution, strong pre-IPO positioning, and sustained post-IPO growth. Leading up to its public debut, CrowdStrike had already demonstrated impressive revenue growth, driven by its innovative cloud-native security platform and a business model that capitalized on increasing cybersecurity threats. The company's ability to generate high annual recurring revenue (ARR) and maintain a strong customer retention rate further solidified investor confidence. By 2025, CrowdStrike's transition from an IPO stock to a market leader reflected its ability to scale operations effectively, maintain consistent revenue growth, and outpace competitors in an evolving industry.

The success of CrowdStrike's IPO was also a reflection of the market appetite for cybersecurity investments at the time. With increasing cyber threats, including high-profile data breaches and nation-state attacks, the demand for advanced security solutions was surging. Investors saw CrowdStrike as a pure-play cybersecurity firm with a differentiated platform, making it an attractive asset in portfolios focused on technology and enterprise security. Additionally, the broader stock market in 2019 was experiencing heightened interest in technology IPOs, setting favorable conditions for a strong debut. CrowdStrike's ability to capitalize on this momentum exemplifies why timing is crucial for IPO success.

CrowdStrike's financial success was rooted in its ability to scale efficiently while maintaining healthy unit economics. The company operated on a subscription-based model, offering software-as-a-service (SaaS) solutions that allowed for predictable revenue streams and higher gross margins. Investors are particularly drawn to companies with a high Rule of 40 score (a measure of revenue growth plus profitability), and CrowdStrike consistently delivered on this metric. The company's customer acquisition cost (CAC) to customer lifetime value (LTV) ratio was also highly favorable, indicating a strong return on investment for new customers.

Institutional investors played a key role in CrowdStrike's post-IPO performance. Strong backing from venture capital and pre-IPO funding rounds provided credibility, while the choice of leading investment banks as underwriters added further validation. When a company attracts significant demand from institutional investors, it signals confidence in its growth trajectory and stability, reducing post-IPO volatility. CrowdStrike benefited from this institutional demand, helping to stabilize share price performance and build long-term investor trust.

To provide greater investor insight, a comparison to other cybersecurity IPOs during the same period would illustrate why CrowdStrike stood out. Other cybersecurity firms, such as Zscaler and Palo Alto Networks, followed different growth strategies. CrowdStrike's cloud-native approach, coupled with its AI-driven detection and prevention capabilities, gave it a competitive advantage. This reinforces the idea that while industry tailwinds can boost an IPO, the true differentiators are business model execution, competitive positioning, and financial discipline.

CrowdStrike's IPO success underscores the importance of aligning key IPO elements—market demand, financial strength, technology differentiation, and institutional backing. Investors evaluating future IPOs should focus on companies with strong ARR growth, a scalable business model, and clear market leadership. CrowdStrike also highlights the importance of looking beyond short-term IPO hype and assessing whether the company can execute a long-term strategic vision that translates into shareholder value.

The difference is clear in examples like CrowdStrike, which continued to beat revenue targets and scale profitably, versus WeWork, where flashy valuation obscured a broken model. In hindsight, CrowdStrike's fundamentals spoke for themselves while WeWork's lacked the financial and governance infrastructure for public scrutiny.

Tapping into high-growth sectors increases IPO appeal, but it does not guarantee success. Cutting-edge solutions and technology attract attention, particularly when companies leverage AI, blockchain, and other transformative innovations. User-centric products that solve tangible, high-impact problems gain stronger traction in public markets. Strong intellectual property and patents create defensible competitive advantages, while financial strength, sustainable margins, high revenue growth, and clear paths to profitability instill confidence. The ability to rapidly expand and redefine an industry fuels long-term investor enthusiasm.

However, successful IPOs do not merely ride trends. They execute. They solve real market needs through disciplined operations, robust financials, strong governance, and scalable business models. Public investors do not reward potential alone. They reward results.

FINAL TAKEAWAYS

For investors, the message is clear:

An IPO is one of the few times you can invest in a company at the inflection point of transformation, but only if you look beyond the pitch deck. The best outcomes go to those who apply rigorous due diligence, analyze fundamentals over narratives, and ignore the noise of hype cycles.

Approach every IPO with a clear investor mindset:

- Is the business model built for scale and sustainability?
- Does the leadership team have a track record of execution under public scrutiny?
- Is the valuation grounded in reality or inflated by private-market optimism?
- Is governance strong, transparent, and shareholder-aligned?

Discipline, not speculation, is the investor's edge. The market will always test every assumption. Companies that thrive post-IPO do so because they have earned investor trust through delivery, not promises. Likewise, investors who build conviction through research, not emotion, are best positioned to capture value over the long-term.

In the end, the IPO process serves as a reality check for both founders and investors. Those who enter the public markets prepared, clear-eyed, and committed to long-term value will endure. Those who chase hype or cut corners will inevitably be exposed.

The ultimate investor skill? Knowing the difference.

CHAPTER 8

The Retail Revolution in IPO Access

A NEW ERA FOR THE EVERYDAY INVESTOR

For decades, IPO investing was a velvet-rope affair, an exclusive domain where allocations were quietly handed to institutional investors, high-net-worth clients, and those with privileged access to underwriter networks. Retail investors weren't just excluded; they were an afterthought. By the time the public could buy in, prices had often surged, and the real upside had already been claimed. But that old playbook is being rewritten.

A convergence of forces, technology, regulation, and investor demand, is dismantling the gatekeeping structures that once defined public offerings. Today, retail investors are not only demanding a seat at the IPO table, but they're also building the tools and ecosystems to claim it. Commission-free trading, real-time research access, and digital-first platforms are redefining what's possible for individual participants. Yet, the path is not without obstacles.

Institutions still control the lion's share of allocations, information asymmetries persist, and many retail investors enter the IPO arena without a clear understanding of how the process works, what signals matter, or how to separate opportunity from hype. This chapter is your guide to that evolving landscape.

We'll explore how retail access to IPOs has changed, why information, not access alone, is the true competitive advantage, and what practical strategies investors can use to participate with clarity and confidence. From cutting-edge tools to research timelines to platform comparisons, we'll equip you with the playbook needed to move from passive observer to informed participant.

In this new era of IPO investing, the difference isn't just in who gets in; it's in how they play once they do.

THE EVOLUTION OF RETAIL ACCESS

Historically, IPO participation was the exclusive domain of institutional investors and high-net-worth individuals. Retail investors lacked access not due to oversight but by design. Participation often required personal relationships with underwriters or multi-million-dollar brokerage accounts.

This began to change in the late 1990s when online brokerages like E*TRADE and TD Waterhouse introduced limited retail IPO access. Still, allocations were small, and the playing field remained steeply tilted.

The cost of exclusion wasn't just theoretical; it was financial. Over the past two decades, many of the most successful public companies delivered their highest returns in the first six to twelve months after IPO. Amazon, Google, Facebook, and Shopify all experienced price surges early in their public life cycles. Retail investors, often restricted from participating at the offering price, were left to buy in at significantly higher valuations, if at all. Understanding this history helps explain the urgency of today's access revolution.

Momentum accelerated post-2008, when the JOBS Act opened new pathways for early-stage company funding. Title III, which went live in 2016, gave rise to equity crowdfunding platforms, enabling broader investor participation.

Today, with the advent of commission-free trading, shortened settlement cycles, and specialized mobile platforms, IPO access for retail investors has improved dramatically. Still, institutions continue to receive 90 percent or more of IPO allocations. The gates are open, but the seats remain limited.

THE INFORMATION ASYMMETRY CHALLENGE

Even when retail investors gain access to an IPO, they face a persistent and critical disadvantage: information.

Institutional investors benefit from:

- Proprietary research and dedicated analyst teams
- Exclusive access to roadshows and private meetings with company leadership
- Deep-rooted professional networks and insider channels
- Advanced data analytics and valuation models powered by AI and machine learning

Retail investors, by contrast, often find themselves evaluating IPOs days or even hours before trading begins, working from only publicly available documents and limited commentary. According to the CFA Institute, institutional investors access three to five times more data points when evaluating IPOs. In technical or emerging sectors, where nuanced insight is vital, this data gap translates into significant outperformance; institutions historically beat retail investors by 30–40 percent in six-month post-IPO returns.

But the asymmetry isn't just about access to more data; it's about context and timing.

Institutions begin their IPO diligence sixty to ninety days before most retail investors even become aware of an offering. They attend roadshows where executives share off-the-record insights, and they use sentiment models and sector positioning tools to contextualize every signal. Retail investors, by contrast, often receive information only after the narrative has already been shaped by institutional consensus.

This gap also extends to behavioral dynamics. Institutions are supported by compliance departments, risk committees, and collective decision-making structures. Retail investors, operating alone, are more susceptible to behavioral biases, overconfidence, FOMO, confirmation bias, and herd behavior. These biases are amplified in IPOs, where media hype and limited data combine to create a fog of speculation.

Understanding these structural differences isn't a cause for discouragement; it's a call to arms.

The good news is that modern tools, platforms, and digital communities are closing the gap. Informed retail investors can now replicate many of the same processes that institutions use if they know where to look and how to think critically. The challenge isn't just to access more information; it's to interpret that information like a professional: with discipline, perspective, and a long-term mindset.

As we move into the next section, we'll explore the practical tools retail investors can use to bridge this gap and how to assemble a modern IPO research stack that rivals institutional workflows.

CHAPTER 8

ESSENTIAL INFORMATION RESOURCES

To bridge the IPO information gap, retail investors must move beyond headlines and hype. The modern investor now has access to a powerful suite of digital tools, some of which were once the exclusive domain of institutions. These platforms don't just provide data; they offer insights, context, and analytical firepower that can fundamentally change how you evaluate an offering.

The key is knowing what tools to use, when to use them, and how to build an efficient research workflow.

DIGITAL RESEARCH PLATFORMS

Modern digital platforms bring pre-IPO intelligence within reach of everyday investors. These tools enable you to analyze company fundamentals, benchmark valuations, and monitor deal pipelines with far greater speed and precision.

- Renaissance Capital's IPO Intelligence provides subscription-based access to analyst-quality research, financial modeling, and valuation data. Their IPO ETF also offers exposure to a curated basket of newly public companies.
- Bloomberg Terminal and FactSet, once the exclusive purview of hedge funds and institutional desks, now offer scaled-down retail packages that include IPO calendars, earnings estimates, and peer analysis tools.
- Alternative data providers like SimilarWeb and Thinknum offer non-traditional datasets, web traffic trends, hiring patterns, and app downloads that

can validate or challenge growth narratives in the S-1 filing.

These platforms form the quantitative backbone of modern IPO research, allowing retail investors to construct evidence-based investment theses instead of relying on speculation or third-party commentary.

CASE STUDY: DEALMAKER'S RETAIL REVOLUTION

DealMaker represents a new generation of platforms fundamentally changing how companies approach public offerings. Founded in 2017 by securities attorneys and fintech experts, it evolved into a comprehensive solution, enabling companies to conduct offerings with significantly higher retail participation.

The platform's key innovation is its information transparency approach:

- *Issuer-direct communication: Companies communicate directly with potential retail investors through compliant messaging systems, reducing information intermediaries.*
- *Interactive offering documents: Static PDFs are transformed into interactive experiences with embedded video and data visualizations that make complex information more accessible.*
- *Real-time allocation transparency: Investors receive continuous updates on allocation status and overall offering progress, eliminating the information blackout that typically disadvantages retail participants.*

- *Post-offering analytics: Retail investors gain access to detailed analytics on shareholder demographics, geographic distribution, and holding patterns—information traditionally available only to company insiders and major institutional investors.*

Recent performance metrics demonstrate its impact: In March 2025 alone, DealMaker processed $96 million in investments from 40,657 individual investors, with retail participation rates of 40-60 percent compared to the 10-15 percent in traditional offerings. This includes facilitating over $66 million from a single issuer within a one-week period, demonstrating the platform's ability to handle high-volume retail participation efficiently.

This approach has translated into meaningful differences:

- *Broader shareholder bases (12,000 + retail shareholders vs. 2,000–3,000 in traditional IPOs)*
- *40 percent lower transaction costs for retail investors*
- *Reduced post-IPO price volatility, challenging conventional wisdom about institutional stability*

DealMaker's model suggests a potential future where technology-enabled direct listings become the norm rather than the exception. By demonstrating that retail-heavy offerings can be compliant and efficient, the platform is helping reshape market expectations around who belongs in an IPO allocation.

COMMUNITY AND SOCIAL INTELLIGENCE

Information isn't just about numbers; it's also about collective insight. Social platforms have become a powerful counterbalance to institutional knowledge, enabling crowdsourced due diligence and real-time sentiment analysis.

- Reddit forums like r/IPO and private Discord servers create collaborative environments where investors dissect S-1 filings, share sector expertise, and flag red flags before they hit the mainstream.
- Commonstock and similar platforms verify users' professional credentials, allowing real-world experts, engineers, physicians, and marketers to weigh in on IPOs in their sectors, adding context that traditional analysts may miss.
- Crowdsourced analysis templates allow dozens or even hundreds of contributors to dissect an IPO collaboratively, covering everything from unit economics and TAM assumptions to lock-up expiration dates.

In this new ecosystem, insight is no longer top-down; it's lateral. Communities bring diverse perspectives, surface hidden insights, and create accountability around IPO narratives.

SEC FILING TOOLS

The IPO prospectus (Form S-1) remains the most powerful source of truth for IPO evaluation, but it's dense, technical, and time-consuming to read. Fortunately, modern tools are making this foundational document far more accessible.

- AI-driven platforms like AlphaSense and Sentieo use natural language processing to extract risk factors, detect linguistic changes in amended filings, and flag anomalies across similar companies.

- Visualization tools transform raw prospectus data into interactive charts, making it easier to understand cap tables, revenue trends, and dilution effects.
- SimpliFi and other plain-language converters translate financial jargon into clear, investor-friendly summaries, ideal for investors seeking fast clarity without sacrificing depth.

Together, these tools empower retail investors to read between the lines, verify company claims, and uncover risks that might otherwise remain hidden.

ACCESSING IPOS: PLATFORM COMPARISON

While gaining access to IPO shares used to require a Rolodex full of banking contacts and a brokerage account with seven figures, today's market offers a growing range of platforms tailored to different types of investors. Understanding where and how to access IPO allocations is essential because access isn't created equal, and neither is the quality of experience across platforms.

Here's how the modern IPO access landscape breaks down across three major categories:

Traditional Brokerages

Established firms like Fidelity, Charles Schwab, and TD Ameritrade remain the most consistent route for investors seeking higher allocation potential, especially in oversubscribed offerings. But they come with high barriers to entry.

- Fidelity provides a robust IPO center, offering prospectus access, calendars, and educational webinars. Clients with accounts above $100,000 typically receive allocations, and high-net-worth investors often receive priority.

- Charles Schwab extends its proprietary Schwab Equity Ratings to IPOs, offering internal valuation and risk rankings. Its Select Client program enhances access for accounts exceeding $500,000.
- TD Ameritrade integrates IPO visibility within its Think or Swim platform, allowing technical traders to evaluate IPOs in the context of broader market momentum and sector performance.

Investor Takeaway

Traditional brokerages may be the only route to allocations in large, institutional-led IPOs, but the asset thresholds and opaque allocation policies require patience and preparation.

Fintech Platforms

Robinhood, SoFi, and Public.com have democratized IPO access, slashing entry requirements and offering mobile-first platforms designed for newer investors. These platforms excel in user experience but often struggle with allocation depth.

- Robinhood's IPO Access offers simplified summaries and interactive explainers of company business models. Allocation is lottery-based and often limited in size, especially for high-demand offerings.
- SoFi Investing incorporates IPO education into its onboarding flow, helping first-time investors understand risks, mechanics, and lock-up periods. SoFi

also penalizes rapid selling with "flipping restrictions," promoting longer-term thinking.

- Public.com integrates Community Sentiment signals, allowing users to see what upcoming IPOs others are watching or favoring, creating a sense of social benchmarking.

Investor Takeaway

Fintech platforms offer the lowest barriers to entry but provide smaller, less frequent allocations. Their strength lies in accessibility and education, not necessarily in early access to top-tier deals.

Specialized IPO Platforms

Built with IPO access as their core function, these platforms aim to optimize every step of the process, from registration to research to allocation tracking.

- ClickIPO connects directly to existing brokerage accounts, offering live alerts, allocation forecasts, and real-time participation tracking.
- Freedom24 provides guaranteed allocations for qualifying users, paired with in-depth pre-IPO research and a suite of long-term investment tools.
- Webull's IPO Center stands out for its balance of usability and transparency, weighting allocation based on factors like account tenure, trading volume, and platform activity, clearly communicating how access is determined.

Investor Takeaway

These platforms are ideal for IPO-focused investors looking to build recurring access over time. While still new compared to legacy brokers, their IPO-first design philosophy is shaping the next wave of digital allocation infrastructure.

TACTICAL APPROACHES FOR INFORMATION ACCESS

Knowing what to look for is only part of the equation. Serious IPO investors must also know when to look, where to look, and how to connect the dots across a fragmented landscape. The advantage no longer lies in who has the most information but in who accesses it most effectively and interprets it with discipline.

BUILD YOUR INFORMATION NETWORK

A well-curated information network gives you early access to insights, deal flow updates, and peer analysis. It also multiplies your capacity to cross-reference claims, discover overlooked signals, and build confidence in your own investment thesis.

- Maintain accounts across multiple IPO platforms, including at least one traditional brokerage, one fintech app, and one IPO-dedicated service. Many platforms provide research access even without requiring a funded account.
- Follow key voices in fintech, investment banking, and equity capital markets on LinkedIn, Twitter (X), and Substack. These include deal syndicate

members, analysts covering pre-IPO firms, and regulatory observers who spot trends before they hit headlines.

- Join vertical-specific investor communities (e.g., biotech Slack groups, fintech Discord servers, or industry-specific Reddit forums) where professionals often discuss IPO-stage companies long before they file.

Pro tip: Create a dedicated RSS feed or watchlist dashboard to consolidate IPO calendars, SEC filings, and press releases into one streamlined view.

MASTER THE INFORMATION TIMELINE

The IPO information cycle is highly structured, but most retail investors only engage at the very end. By shifting your attention upstream, you gain a clearer view of the company's trajectory and can develop your investment thesis before the market narrative takes hold.

- 6–12 months pre-filing: Monitor for key signals like CFO or GC appointments, late-stage venture rounds, and brand refreshes. These moves often precede an IPO filing.
- Initial S-1 filing: This is your first look at the company's financials, business model, and risk factors. Download and analyze the prospectus as early as possible.
- S-1 amendments: These often contain critical changes, revised financials, updated risk disclosures, or valuation adjustments in response to market feedback.

- Roadshow period (2–3 weeks pre-pricing): Pay attention to analyst commentary, media interviews, and institutional sentiment. This is when deal momentum becomes visible.
- Pricing window (24–48 hours pre-trading): Final offering price and share count are set. Use this window to adjust expectations and prepare your post-IPO monitoring strategy.

By mapping your due diligence process to this timeline, you increase your odds of identifying red flags, valuation mismatches, or opportunity gaps before the broader market catches on.

USE AI-POWERED TOOLS

Artificial intelligence is changing the game in IPO research. Where institutions once relied on armies of analysts, individual investors can now deploy AI to process dense filings, identify patterns, and benchmark data in minutes.

- Natural language processing (NLP) tools can detect hedging language, inconsistencies, or sentiment shifts across S-1 and S-1/A filings.
- Allocation simulators use historical platform behavior, account size, and deal size to estimate your likely IPO allocation, helping you set realistic expectations.
- Machine learning models aggregate third-party data (e.g., SimilarWeb traffic, App Store rankings) and align it with company claims to validate or challenge growth projections.

These tools don't just save time; they help retail investors ask better questions and focus on what matters most.

THE FUTURE OF RETAIL INFORMATION ACCESS

The landscape of IPO access is evolving rapidly, and the changes ahead may be even more transformational than those we've seen over the past decade. As retail participation in capital markets continues to rise, regulators, platforms, and issuers alike are being pushed to rethink long-held assumptions about who deserves access and how information is distributed.

The SEC has signaled its intent to address information disparities that favor institutions, with proposed reforms aimed at increasing retail access to key stages of the IPO process, such as roadshows, analyst briefings, and post-filing data updates. While still in development, these reforms suggest a future in which selective information sharing becomes less acceptable and transparency becomes a regulatory expectation, not a value-add.

Internationally, progressive models are already shaping new norms. Hong Kong mandates minimum IPO allocations for retail investors, while several European exchanges have adopted digital-first frameworks that streamline investor onboarding, education, and document access. These global benchmarks are influencing U.S. market infrastructure and regulatory thinking.

On the technology front, blockchain-based allocation systems offer the promise of near-instant transparency, enabling investors to track offering progress, share distribution, and account eligibility in real-time. Meanwhile, AI-powered research platforms are accelerating the ability to decode S-1 filings, extract sentiment trends, and even simulate post-IPO performance scenarios based on historical analogs.

Looking ahead, tomorrow's retail investors will demand:

- Interactive prospectuses with embedded videos, visual data, and plain-English explanations
- Mobile-native platforms that deliver research, alerts, and allocation participation in one seamless experience
- Transparent allocation logic that replaces opaque "invite-only" policies with merit- or activity-based models
- Community-integrated insights, where peer sentiment and expert perspectives are layered into decision-making tools

Companies that proactively meet these expectations will not only benefit from broader investor interest, but they'll likely see more stable shareholder bases, reduced post-IPO volatility, and stronger long-term support. In this new environment, transparency is no longer just good governance; it's a competitive advantage.

The future of IPO access is not just about opening the door wider; it's about reshaping the architecture of that door entirely.

ACTION PLAN: PRACTICAL STEPS FOR BETTER IPO ACCESS

For retail investors, better IPO access isn't just about being in the right place; it's about being prepared. The following steps will help position you strategically across platforms, tools, and timelines while developing the habits that separate informed participants from speculative traders.

1. Diversify Your Access Points

Create accounts with at least one traditional brokerage (e.g., Fidelity), one fintech app (e.g., Robinhood or SoFi), and one IPO-specific platform (e.g., ClickIPO or Webull). Some offer early research access even before you've funded the account.

2. Set Smart Alerts

Use IPO calendars and watchlists from sources like Nasdaq, Renaissance Capital, and MarketWatch to track companies in your sectors of interest. Look for early indicators like funding rounds, regulatory filings, and key executive hires.

3. Build a Centralized Dashboard

Combine your top research tools into a single view. Include:

- SEC EDGAR for filings and amendments
- Renaissance Capital for calendar and institutional analysis
- Alternative data from SimilarWeb or Thinknum
- Sentiment insights from Reddit or Twitter feeds

4. Join High-Signal Communities

Contribute to niche groups on Reddit (e.g., r/IPO), Discord, LinkedIn, or Commonstock, where collective diligence happens in real-time. These groups often flag developments before they hit mainstream channels.

5. Use AI Tools Strategically

During active IPO periods, activate free trials of tools like AlphaSense, Sentieo, or SimpliFi to evaluate filings quickly and identify risks. Use NLP outputs, risk-factor heatmaps, and comparative benchmarks to validate your thesis.

6. Express Early Interest

Many allocation models favor early sign-ups or expressions of interest. If a platform allows it, indicate your interest in offerings before final pricing—this can improve your odds of getting shares, especially in time-sensitive or overallocated deals.

7. Track Your Performance Like a Portfolio Manager

Maintain a record of:

- Allocation success rates across platforms
- Actual vs. expected allocations
- Post-IPO price behavior and holding outcomes
- Research accuracy and platform reliability

This feedback loop will help refine your approach, highlight blind spots, and evolve your personal IPO playbook over time. The most successful retail IPO investors aren't necessarily the earliest or loudest; they're the most prepared.

CHAPTER 8

FINAL TAKEAWAYS

IPO access is no longer solely a question of who you know. Today, it's about what you know, when you know it, and how strategically you apply that knowledge.

The retail revolution isn't just about opening doors; it's about transforming the map. Allocation systems may remain imperfect, but the true battleground is shifting to information: who sees the signals first, who can decode them accurately, and who has the discipline to act with intention rather than emotion.

We are witnessing a fundamental shift in capital markets, a transition from privilege to preparation. For retail investors who are willing to engage, study, question, and collaborate, the IPO market is no longer a gated arena ruled by institutional gatekeepers.

It's a frontier.

And like any frontier, it favors those who are ready to:

- Think independently
- Use modern tools with confidence
- Show up early, ask better questions, and demand transparency
- Build an edge, not by chasing hype, but by mastering insight

As the walls around IPO information continue to come down, a new class of investor is emerging informed, empowered, and proactive. The opportunity isn't just to participate; it's to shape what access looks like for the next generation.

The future of IPO investing belongs to those who know where to look and what to do when they find it.

CHAPTER 9

IPO Trading Strategies for the Knowledgeable Investor

Sophisticated U.S. retail investors have grown increasingly skilled in direct stock ownership and trading strategies. Yet, IPO trading stands apart, requiring specialized knowledge and a distinct approach. The lack of historical data limited financial visibility, and an early-stage reliance on narratives over fundamentals make IPOs unique and often volatile.

This chapter offers experienced retail investors actionable insights to navigate the distinct challenges and opportunities of IPO trading. It focuses on how to interpret limited company data, separate genuine growth potential from promotional hype, and identify meaningful signals within IPO registration statements. Understanding these nuances can help investors manage risk and sharpen decision-making around new public listings.

IPO shares come to market without trading history, and early sentiment can swing wildly, fueled by institutional demand, media attention, and underwriter influence. In the short-term, momentum often trumps fundamentals. Retail investors must tread carefully, particularly when institutional players dominate the initial price action.

PSYCHOLOGICAL PREPARATION — MASTERING THE MENTAL GAME OF IPO TRADING

IPOs introduce a unique psychological dimension that can challenge even the most seasoned investors. Many of the most spectacular IPO losses stem not from flawed business models but from investor overreaction—buying too high, selling too soon, or clinging to positions in defiance of clear signals. The market rarely punishes lack of knowledge as swiftly as it punishes lack of emotional control. Limited historical data, intense media coverage, and sudden price swings create a charged environment where emotions can easily eclipse rational analysis.

One of the key challenges of IPO trading is the anxiety caused by information asymmetry. Established companies provide years of operating and price data, whereas IPOs do not. This absence makes it easy for investors to fill the gaps with hype or speculation instead of facts. In turn, this leads to reliance on the company's "story" to guide decisions, a phenomenon known as narrative-driven investing. When financial details are sparse, investors often gravitate toward narratives that affirm their enthusiasm, ignoring risks that don't fit the storyline.

This vulnerability is amplified by FOMO, the fear of missing out. The excitement of being "early" in an IPO can cloud judgment, enticing investors to participate without adequately weighing risks or valuation. Compounding this is time compression stress, as prices can swing wildly in the early moments of trading. Under these circumstances, impulsive decisions often replace rational strategies. Think of the IPO market as an echo chamber inside a pressure cooker. At the moment of debut, investors are flooded with headlines, forecasts, and hype, but little proof. In this vacuum, emotions become the loudest signal.

Psychological biases become especially acute during IPO trading. Anchoring bias leads investors to view the IPO price as a fair benchmark, regardless of underlying fundamentals. Outcome bias tricks investors into believing that early price movements reflect intrinsic value when they often reflect speculative sentiment. Herd behavior further distorts judgment, as institutional activity and social proof create the illusion of legitimacy. And recency bias may lead investors to extrapolate the success or failure of recent IPOs in similar sectors onto the latest offering.

To manage these psychological pressures, investors should adopt a clear mental framework. Before the trade, define your entry and exit strategy with specific technical or fundamental criteria. Right-size your position to account for heightened volatility. Consider walking through multiple "what if" scenarios to mentally prepare for outcomes ranging from sudden surges to disappointing declines. During trading, step away from your screen when you feel pressure to act impulsively. Practice cognitive diffusion; label those feelings as thoughts, not facts. Journaling your decisions and emotional states can help identify patterns over time.

After a trade, assess whether you followed your process, regardless of profit or loss. Evaluate what triggered your strongest reactions and track your ability to stay calm under pressure.

Developing discipline in IPO trading isn't just beneficial; it's essential to long-term performance. Investors who treat psychology as a core component of their trading edge, alongside financial analysis, position themselves to thrive not just on day one but for years to come.

OPEN MARKET TRADING STRATEGIES

For most retail investors, the opening bell of an IPO marks the first real chance to participate. But unlike institutions, they're entering a market already in motion, often distorted by hype, liquidity mismatches, and strategic price support from underwriters. In this environment, strategy isn't optional; it's a survival tool. Selecting a post-IPO approach that matches your risk tolerance, temperament, and time horizon is essential to preserving capital and seizing opportunity.

Short-term traders often aim to ride the "first-day pop," buying shares shortly after they debut. This strategy demands rapid execution and clear exit rules, as price action is typically volatile and unforgiving. Without discipline, it's easy to get caught buying into a spike that fades before the trade can be closed. Medium-term swing traders take a different approach, waiting for the initial excitement to cool. Early profit-taking can create more favorable entry points, especially when the company's fundamentals or sector outlook remain strong. Trend followers, on the other hand, wait for clear technical confirmation. They look for the stock to break above prior resistance on strong volume, signaling institutional accumulation and the start of a new upward trend.

Some investors look beyond chart patterns altogether, focusing on sectors with macro or regulatory tailwinds, such as AI, biotech, or clean energy. These thematic investors align conviction with timing, combining market momentum with broader economic narratives. Meanwhile, long-term investors take the slowest route. They often wait weeks, even months, until trading stabilizes and new data becomes available, preferring clarity over noise and evidence over emotion.

For those who missed out on the IPO allocation, there are key signals that can suggest better entry points.

Lock-up expirations, typically around 180 days after the IPO, often trigger insider selling, creating temporary pressure on share prices. These moments can offer contrarian opportunities, especially if the company's long-term outlook remains strong. Early earnings reports and analyst coverage are other inflection points when sentiment and valuation may abruptly shift. Traders should also stay alert to volume spikes, which often signal institutional involvement. And while technical tools like moving averages or RSI aren't crystal balls, they can help confirm whether a stock is gaining traction or losing it.

In IPO trading, clarity beats urgency. While institutional investors may shape the initial landscape, retail investors who master post-IPO strategy can carve out meaningful advantages, not by chasing the crowd but by entering with intent, precision, and a plan.

OVER-ALLOTMENT AND STABILIZATION

One often overlooked feature of IPO pricing is the green shoe option, formally known as the over-allotment clause. This provision allows underwriters to sell up to 15 percent more shares than initially offered, giving them flexibility to manage volatility and stabilize the stock post-listing. If the stock price dips below the IPO offer price, underwriters may repurchase shares to prevent a steeper decline. If demand exceeds expectations and the stock trades well above the offer price, they may exercise the full green shoe, effectively increasing supply to meet market appetite.

To the trained eye, the green shoe isn't just a technical clause; it's a signal. How and when it's used provides insight into the strength and sustainability of IPO demand. When a company's stock trades consistently above the offer price without triggering buybacks, it suggests genuine institutional interest and market confidence. Conversely, when underwriters intervene early to stabilize falling prices, it can indicate overpricing or soft demand masked by early marketing.

Retail investors don't have direct access to these stabilization tools, but they can benefit by interpreting the clues left behind. Regulatory filings in the first thirty days, particularly Form 8-K updates and trading volume data, can reveal how actively underwriters are managing the stock. Spikes in volume or sudden rebounds near the offering price often reflect stabilization activity. In cases where the full green shoe is exercised, it's often a strong signal of early momentum and institutional support, especially when accompanied by rising volume and upward price action.

For investors watching from the sidelines, green shoe activity is one of the few transparent markers of behind-the-scenes market dynamics. It offers a rare glimpse into how the IPO is being managed and whether the early price action reflects organic demand or carefully orchestrated support. In a market where perception can move faster than fundamentals, that knowledge is power.

MOMENTUM VS. FUNDAMENTALS: UNDERSTANDING THE PLAYERS

Navigating the IPO market isn't just about analyzing the company; it's about understanding the players. Each phase of trading reflects the actions of different investor groups, each with their own time horizon, strategy, and signals. The earliest activity is often driven by momentum traders, short-term participants who seek to capitalize on sharp price movements. They rely on technical indicators such as moving averages, RSI, or MACD, and react quickly to volume spikes and trend reversals. Their trades can move prices fast, but their positions are fragile, turning on a dime when momentum fades.

In contrast, fundamental investors adopt a longer view. They wait for the dust to settle and focus on the company's earnings trajectory, margin potential, insider ownership, and competitive moat. Their advantage lies in patience and conviction. Rather than react to every price fluctuation, they enter when valuations make sense and remain steady through early volatility, betting on what the company can become rather than how it performs on day one.

Sitting atop the hierarchy are institutional investors. These players move methodically, backed by deep research teams, proprietary data, and flexible capital. Their presence may not be immediately visible, but their trades can quietly shape price action through sustained accumulation or exit activity. While they rarely chase headlines, their influence builds over time, creating invisible currents that drive longer-term trends.

For retail traders, the goal isn't to outmaneuver institutions but to read the water. Subtle shifts in volume, unusually consistent price support, or breakouts that hold on high volume can suggest institutional footprints. Learning to recognize when large players are building or unwinding positions gives retail investors a valuable edge. In a market shaped by rhythm as much as reason, understanding who's behind the movement can often matter more than the movement itself.

MANAGING FIRST-WEEK VOLATILITY

Few trading environments test investor discipline like the first week of an IPO. Here, volatility isn't just expected; it's baked in. Thin floats, valuation uncertainty, and speculative demand combine to create sharp price swings that can mislead even the most experienced traders. For newly public companies in hot sectors, where narrative often outpaces data, the early days become a battleground of hype and hesitation.

Surviving this environment requires more than courage; it demands preparation. Successful traders don't commit their capital all at once. Instead, they scale into positions, probing the market's strength while protecting against sudden reversals. They set stop-loss orders not as signs of fear but as anchors of discipline, boundaries that protect long-term capital from short-term chaos. Trailing stops also play a role. These dynamic safeguards help lock in gains while giving trades room to breathe. The best traders know that volatility can be a gift, but only when position sizes are small enough to keep emotions in check.

Emotional discipline is where strategy becomes an edge. Volatility triggers excitement, and excitement clouds thinking. Think of IPO trading like surfing a breaking wave; the moment you lose balance, the wave owns you. Following a pre-set plan with defined entry points, exit targets, and risk limits helps you stay centered amid the churn. Step away from the screen when you feel the urge to act impulsively. Don't chase losses in the heat of the moment; pause, reflect, and return with perspective. Every trade is data, and every mistake is feedback. Those who learn fastest, not react fastest, win the long game in IPO trading.

CAPITALIZING ON LOCK-UP EXPIRATIONS AND EARNINGS REPORTS

While IPOs begin with fanfare, their real tests arrive weeks or months later, when insiders are free to sell, and the company must face its first public earnings report. These moments are not just time-sensitive; they're reality checks. Lock-up expirations and early earnings calls strip away the marketing veneer and expose how investors truly value the business. For traders and long-term investors alike, these inflection points offer rare opportunities to gauge conviction, recalibrate entries, or capitalize on overreactions.

The expiration of the IPO lock-up period is one such moment. When insiders, often holding large blocks of shares, are allowed to sell, the sudden shift in supply can depress prices, especially in companies with a low float. Traders anticipating this may take short positions one to two weeks in advance, expecting a wave of selling. Others wait five to seven days after the event to evaluate how the market absorbs the pressure. If the stock stabilizes on declining volume and finds support at key technical levels, it may offer a more compelling long entry than the IPO itself.

Some traders approach this volatility using options. Straddles, simultaneously buying calls and puts, allow participation in either direction, provided the move is large enough. This strategy can be particularly effective when uncertainty is high, and the magnitude of the reaction is more predictable than the direction.

Earnings reports carry a different weight. The first quarterly report is the company's first real chance to prove or disprove the IPO narrative. A strong showing, with outsized revenue growth or margin expansion, can send the stock soaring. A miss, especially on guidance, can lead to swift and steep declines. But context matters. In tech, metrics like user growth and R&D investment are often more closely scrutinized than profits. In biotech, a single clinical milestone or FDA comment can outweigh financials altogether.

Occasionally, these events occur close together. When earnings precede a lock-up, a strong report might justify a long position, though hedging with puts can protect against post-lock-up selling pressure. When the lock-up comes first, a short position ahead of the expiration may be warranted, followed by reassessment in the run-up to earnings.

These aren't just tactics; they're signals. How a stock behaves around lock-ups and earnings reveals institutional sentiment, leadership credibility, and whether the market is still buying the story. For investors who understand these rhythms, volatility becomes less a threat and more a roadmap.

CASE STUDIES: UBER, FACEBOOK, AND BEYOND MEAT: LOCK-UP EXPIRATION OUTCOMES

Lock-up expirations represent a critical inflection point for newly public companies, often triggering substantial volatility. While these events are frequently viewed as routine post-IPO mechanics, the data tells a more complex story: outcomes are driven not only by technical selling pressure but by a combination of float dynamics, insider behavior, market sentiment, and company fundamentals. The cases of Uber, Facebook, and Beyond Meat offer valuable insight into how these forces interact and how investors can navigate them with greater foresight.

Uber (2019): Prolonged Decline Amid Weak Fundamentals

- *Lock-up expiration date: November 6, 2019*
- *Shares released: 763 million, doubling the public float*

In the lead-up to its lock-up expiration, Uber's stock experienced significant pressure. Shares fell 17 percent in the four trading days before November 6, compounded by Q3 2019 results released two days prior. While Uber beat revenue expectations, it failed to stem investor concerns over a $1.2 billion quarterly loss and persistent cash burn.

On expiration day, the stock dropped 3.85 percent, closing at $26.90. The decline continued to $25.58 by November 22, down 38.6 percent from post-IPO highs.

Key Drivers:

- *Float size: Over 900 million shares flooded the market, overwhelming the average daily trading volume of approximately 9.9 million shares.*
- *Insider sentiment: Early backers, including GV and SoftBank, signaled intent to sell, citing doubts about Uber's path to profitability.*
- *Market sentiment: Short interest spiked to 7.8 percent of the float pre-expiration, indicating elevated bearish bets.*

Uber's lock-up outcome illustrates how structural selling pressure and weak fundamentals can collide, accelerating price erosion even in the absence of a major news catalyst.

Facebook (2012): Gradual Erosion After IPO Debacle

- *Lock-up expiration dates: Staggered between August 2012 and May 2013*
- *Largest expiration: November 14, 2012 (773 million shares, including Mark Zuckerberg's 504 million)*

Facebook entered the public markets under immense scrutiny, following a botched IPO and concerns over mobile monetization. By August 2012, the stock had already declined 48 percent from its $38 IPO price. The first lock-up expiration on August 16 triggered a 6 percent drop.

Yet, on November 14, Facebook rallied 10.3 percent, largely due to Mark Zuckerberg's public commitment not to sell his shares. Despite the rally, shares remained 48 percent below the IPO price, and it was not until late 2013, after tangible improvements in mobile ad revenue, that a full recovery began.

Key Drivers:

- *Technical factors: IPO execution flaws and a $104 billion initial valuation severely damaged early investor confidence.*
- *Insider restraint: Zuckerberg's decision not to sell shares helped temporarily stabilize sentiment.*
- *Earnings impact: Q3 2012 results, released October 24, sparked a 22 percent rally and restored some confidence in the business model.*

Facebook's experience highlights how early missteps can create prolonged headwinds but also how strong leadership signals and improving fundamentals can support recovery.

Beyond Meat (2019): Sharp Drop Followed by Recovery

- *Lock-up expiration date: October 29, 2019*
- *Shares released: 48.6 million, representing 80 percent of total shares*

Investor anxiety over insider selling culminated in a 24 percent decline on the expiration day. This followed an earlier secondary offering in July, when 3.5 million shares were sold at $160, a clear profit-taking signal.

Despite an initial drawdown of 50 percent from its July peak ($234.90 to $81.45), Beyond Meat rebounded to $110 by late 2019. The recovery was driven by strong Q3 performance, with $92 million in revenue (up 250 percent year-over-year) and speculation around a potential partnership with McDonald's.

Key Drivers:

- *Fundamentals: Revenue growth and market enthusiasm for plant-based products helped offset insider selling concerns.*
- *Insider actions: Kleiner Perkins sold 2.1 million shares post-expiration, while CEO Ethan Brown held firm, reinforcing confidence.*
- *Market sentiment: Short interest remained relatively low at 30 percent of float, especially when compared to Uber.*

Beyond Meat's outcome illustrates how robust fundamentals and executive alignment can absorb technical selling pressure and restore investor trust.

Key Takeaways for Investors

These three cases show that lock-up expirations are not standalone events. They are accelerants shaped by broader dynamics:

- *Float size matters: Uber and Facebook saw outsized volatility due to massive increases in tradable shares, while Beyond Meat's more limited float helped contain damage.*
- *Insider restraint provides stability: Zuckerberg's hold and Beyond Meat's CEO commitment proved valuable in easing panic.*
- *Fundamentals drive the long-term narrative: Beyond Meat recovered on strong growth, while Uber's losses deepened its decline.*
- *Earnings timing influences perception: Uber's Q3 earnings, released just before expiration, failed*

to reassure investors. In contrast, Beyond Meat's results served as a buffer.

For investors, monitoring lock-up schedules is essential, but understanding the context surrounding them is critical. Float dynamics, insider intentions, market sentiment, and operational performance all converge at these moments. Those who do their homework are far better positioned to separate opportunity from risk.

RISK MANAGEMENT: THE FOUNDATION OF EVERY TRADE

In the chaos of IPO volatility, risk management is your compass, your parachute, and your insurance policy. It is not optional. It is the foundation upon which every strategy must be built. Without it, even the most promising setup becomes an invitation to overreach, and overreach is how traders go broke. Most trading failures don't come from picking the wrong stock. They come from staying too long, sizing too large, or acting without a plan when things go sideways.

The simplest form of protection is the stop-loss. This isn't just a technical tool; it's a boundary. It tells the market where your risk ends and your capital preservation begins. Position sizing is equally critical. If your risk tolerance is $100 and your stop-loss is $5 per share, your trade size should be twenty shares, no more. Let the math dictate your aggression, not the moment.

IPOs are notoriously illiquid in their early days. Avoid names trading under 500,000 shares a day. Thin liquidity magnifies slippage and limits exit options, especially when volatility spikes. No single IPO should dominate your portfolio. Limit exposure to 10 to 15 percent of total capital, allowing room for flexibility, adjustment, and psychological clarity.

Risk rules don't prevent bold trades; they make bold trades survivable. They create the structure necessary to take advantage of opportunity without being consumed by it. They allow you to play the long game because, without risk control, there is no long game. In IPO trading, risk isn't something to manage after the fact; it's something to design into your process, before the trade, not during it. Master this, and you earn the right to stay in the game long enough to win it.

FINAL TAKEAWAYS

IPO trading is not just fast; it's loud, erratic, and unforgiving. It rewards precision but punishes hesitation. For the unprepared, it's chaos. For the disciplined, it's an opportunity. Stepping into this market feels like entering a high-stakes arena, with every headline amplified, every move scrutinized, and every tick loaded with emotion. But beneath the surface, where the noise fades and patterns emerge, lies an edge for those who know how to look.

Success in this space isn't about chasing hype or predicting sentiment; it's about showing up prepared, with a process, a framework, and a clear sense of your own tolerance for risk. It's about knowing when to act and when to wait, when to lean in and when to let the market speak. Throughout this chapter, we've explored how to read the IPO registration statement with discernment, how to decode institutional signals, and how to navigate price action with conviction and caution.

No single strategy fits every IPO. Some names demand agility. Others reward patience. The key is knowing your own profile as an investor, your goals, your blind spots, and your natural rhythm. By ring-fencing your exposure, balancing short-term trades with long-term conviction, and learning to recognize institutional footprints, you transform the IPO process from speculation into strategy.

As an informed investor, your role isn't to guess the future; it's to prepare for it. IPOs offer fresh ground. And for those who approach them with discipline, insight, and humility, they can become a powerful part of a broader investment playbook. This isn't about being early; it's about being ready.

CHAPTER 10

Special Situations - SPACs, Direct Listings, Regulation A+, and Alternative IPO Structures

For decades, the path to public markets was narrow, ritualized, and controlled by a handful of gatekeepers. Companies that wished to go public had one real option: the traditional IPO. It was a system rooted in institutional access, underwriter discretion, and a playbook that hadn't meaningfully changed in generations. But today, that landscape has fractured and evolved.

SPACs, direct listings, and Regulation A+ offerings have emerged not just as alternatives but as strategic instruments for companies with different needs, timelines, and audiences. These structures represent a broader shift in capital formation, one driven by technology, transparency, and a rebalancing of power between private issuers and public investors.

For investors, these "special situations" present opportunity and complexity. They break the mold of conventional IPOs, creating windows for asymmetric upside but also demanding sharper analysis, deeper diligence, and a stronger grasp of structure-specific risk.

In this chapter, we'll demystify these alternative routes to the public markets. We'll examine how each structure works, what differentiates the winners from the rest, and how to assess them not just as speculative plays but as potential cornerstones of a dynamic, forward-leaning investment strategy.

Because in a market increasingly shaped by innovation and disruption, understanding special situations isn't optional; it's essential.

SPACS: A JOURNEY FROM OBSCURITY TO HYPE AND BACK

SPACs (Special Purpose Acquisition Companies) have been around for over thirty years, emerging in the 1980s as vehicles for speculative industries like oil and gas exploration. Their popularity fluctuated, with notable declines during the dot-com bubble and the 2008 financial crisis before resurging in 2019. Initially conceived as vehicles targeting smaller private firms that struggled with the rigorous demands of conventional IPOs, SPACs evolved dramatically during the pandemic-driven market frenzy of 2020–2021. Suddenly, these once-obscure financial structures became mainstream darlings, capturing the imagination and capital of both Wall Street and Main Street. SPAC sponsors ranged from seasoned hedge fund managers to celebrities and sports icons, adding a veneer of glamour to the investment process.

Investors were drawn to SPACs primarily due to their perceived built-in safety mechanism: each SPAC unit typically launched at around $10, bundled with fractional warrants, giving investors the option to redeem their initial investment if the chosen merger target proved unappealing. This structure offered a compelling mix of risk mitigation and speculative upside, fueling widespread interest. In practice, SPAC mergers varied widely in outcomes. Some surged spectacularly, generating extraordinary short-term returns in sectors such as technology, electric vehicles, fintech, and biotechnology, areas investors associated with transformative potential and rapid growth. Others faltered dramatically, burdened by unrealistic forecasts, lackluster execution, or sponsor inexperience.

What many investors overlooked in their initial enthusiasm was that the SPAC structure itself wasn't a panacea. The real determinants of long-term success remained fundamentals, operational expertise, and sponsor alignment with shareholder interests. For instance, while high-profile SPAC mergers such as DraftKings and IonQ demonstrated clear strategic vision and strong execution, cautionary tales like Nikola Motors highlighted how unchecked optimism and insufficient due diligence could rapidly deflate investor expectations and valuations.

From an investor perspective, understanding SPACs requires more than superficial knowledge of their mechanics. It demands meticulous analysis of sponsor credibility, transparent assessment of target company fundamentals, and skepticism toward overly aggressive forecasts. Moreover, investors must closely examine deal terms, such as sponsor compensation arrangements, lockup periods, and warrant structures, to gauge the real economic alignment between sponsors and public shareholders.

Ultimately, the SPAC journey underscores a timeless lesson in investment markets: while novel financial vehicles can provide unique opportunities, they do not alter the fundamental rules of prudent investing. Careful diligence, critical thinking, and disciplined valuation remain essential, particularly when market sentiment swings from exuberance back to rationality.

WHY SOME SPACS WORK

While the SPAC structure gained notoriety for its uneven outcomes, select deals have demonstrated that when the right ingredients align, compelling fundamentals, credible sponsors, and strategic timing, the result can be transformative for investors.

- DraftKings: Capitalized on favorable regulatory momentum in online sports betting, rapidly scaling its user base and monetizing a shifting legal landscape. The company's strong brand recognition, robust revenue streams, and data-driven marketing engine positioned it as a clear category leader. Importantly, DraftKings showcased how a SPAC could serve as a springboard for an already proven business, rather than a lifeline for speculative ventures.
- Intuitive Machines: Emerged as a standout in the post-SPAC bubble era by securing high-value NASA contracts and delivering tangible progress in lunar landing systems and space technology. The company offered real assets, real contracts, and a credible path to recurring revenue, countering the narrative that SPACs are solely vehicles for pre-revenue moonshots.
- IonQ: A quantum computing pioneer that attracted attention for its scientific credibility and partnerships with leading research institutions and hyperscalers. While the business remains early-stage, IonQ's SPAC route allowed patient capital to engage with frontier technology at a pre-hockey-stick moment, with clear milestones and measurable progress indicators.

These success stories reveal a critical distinction: the SPAC itself is not the investment; it's merely the wrapper. What lies within, the business fundamentals, leadership quality, strategic market position, and timing, drives outcomes. Each of these companies entered the public markets with more than a story; they brought executional proof points, traction in regulated or emerging sectors, and leadership teams capable of operating under public market scrutiny.

From an investor standpoint, what sets these SPACs apart is that they weren't just capitalizing on market hype; they were businesses with high-conviction theses, where the SPAC structure simply offered a faster or more flexible path to liquidity. For discerning investors, the lesson is clear: successful SPAC opportunities often mimic the characteristics of strong IPOs. That means doing the hard work, evaluating revenue quality, market size, partnership pipelines, and capital allocation discipline before the ticker goes live.

When properly aligned, SPACs can unlock access to breakthrough technologies and fast-evolving sectors earlier than traditional IPO pipelines might allow. But that access only translates into returns when paired with rigorous diligence and a firm grasp of where value is actually being created.

MODERN SPAC ANALYSIS

Successful SPAC investing begins with understanding that the real bet is not on the structure; it's on the details. Each SPAC is a unique transaction with distinct variables, and investors must approach them with the same rigor they would apply to any complex equity deal. Here's how to break it down:

- Sponsor Credibility: The sponsor team is the cornerstone of a SPAC's potential. Look for sponsors with deep domain expertise, a track record of building or operating successful businesses, and, crucially, skin in the game. Sponsor alignment through personal capital investment is a key signal of confidence and accountability. Reputational risk also plays a role; high-caliber sponsors are less likely to pursue questionable targets that could damage their brand in future deals.
- Target Fundamentals: Flashy pitch decks and bold claims don't create value; cash flows, growth metrics, and market defensibility do. Prioritize companies with verifiable traction: actual revenue, customer adoption, signed contracts, and a clear competitive moat. Discount deals that lean heavily on projections without supporting data. In sectors like biotech or deep tech, milestone-based progress and third-party validation (e.g., regulatory approvals, commercial pilots, or key partnerships) are essential.
- Deal Structure: The architecture of the transaction can dramatically influence investor outcomes. Reasonable valuations relative to public peers are a must, but so is the presence of sophisticated PIPE investors who typically conduct their own deep diligence and serve as a vote of institutional confidence. Watch for red flags like excessive warrant dilution, misaligned incentives, or structures that over reward sponsors regardless of long-term performance. Favor deals with performance-based earnouts, extended sponsor lockups, and transparent financial modeling.

- Post-Merger Strategy: A successful de-SPAC doesn't end at the merger; it starts there. Understand the game plan for building long-term shareholder value. Are there clear post-merger growth initiatives? Will the company need to raise additional capital soon, and under what terms? Monitor the timing of insider lockup expirations, which often trigger increased volatility. Analyst coverage is another factor; lack of visibility can limit institutional engagement. A thoughtful post-merger IR strategy, including transparent guidance and milestone tracking, signals maturity.

From an investor's perspective, this framework is about discipline over excitement. SPACs can offer asymmetric upside, but only when structure, sponsor, and strategy align. In a post-2021 environment of heightened regulatory scrutiny and investor skepticism, deals must pass a higher bar. Applying this analytical lens separates speculative plays from genuine opportunities and positions you to act, not react, when quality emerges.

BEYOND TRADITIONAL IPOS: DIRECT LISTINGS

Direct listings have emerged as a credible alternative to the traditional IPO, not just for their elegance but for what they fundamentally reject. No underwriters. No arbitrary pricing. No sweetheart allocations to institutional insiders. In a direct listing, existing shareholders, founders, employees, and early investors simply bring their equity to the public market and let demand set the price. Its capital formation is stripped of artifice and gatekeeping.

This shift represents more than cost savings. It's a philosophical realignment, one that trusts market mechanisms over managed narratives. Companies that choose this route are often signaling strength; they don't need to sell a story to Wall Street bankers or manufacture demand through allocation scarcity. They're confident in the fundamentals and willing to let the open market decide what they're worth.

But direct listings come with real tradeoffs that sophisticated investors must navigate carefully.

TRADEOFFS OF DIRECT LISTINGS

- No Stabilization Mechanisms: Unlike traditional IPOs, Direct listings rely on market-driven price discovery during the opening auction, facilitated by a designated market maker (DMM), which helps balance supply and demand. That means early volatility is not just possible; it's expected. Sharp price swings can occur in the first hours or days as price discovery plays out in real-time.
- Insider Liquidity Pressure: Since there are no lockups unless voluntarily imposed, insiders are free to sell on day one. Heavy selling can send negative signals about insider confidence, even if the motivation is simply liquidity, not doubt.

These risks are not disqualifiers; they are invitations to deeper analysis. Direct listings reveal truths early. You're watching the market digest information without filters or stabilizers. That transparency, when understood properly, is an edge.

CHAPTER 10

THE DIRECT LISTING PLAYBOOK

For investors, the key is not to react but to read the tape strategically. Here's how to approach these listings:

- Observe Early Volatility Without Chasing: The first trades are often irrational, driven by pent-up demand or speculative enthusiasm. Let the market find its footing. In many cases, the price settles into a range within the first few sessions that better reflects fundamental value.
- Monitor Insider Transactions (Form 4 Filings): Watch for who's selling and at what volume. Not all selling is created equal. Founders cashing out a small portion of long-held equity is expected. If C-suite executives or board members offload large stakes, that's a flag worth investigating.
- Track Institutional Conviction (13F Filings): These filings are delayed but invaluable. Look for whether long-term funds are accumulating shares in the weeks and months after the listing. The presence of quality capital is a strong validator of future potential.
- Read Volume and Float Dynamics: Many direct listings have constrained float initially. Combine that with heavy interest, and you have conditions ripe for price dislocations. Understand the ownership structure: who holds what and when they might sell. That helps anticipate liquidity events before they impact price.

Direct listings are not for passive investors. They require patience, a high tolerance for early volatility, and a commitment to doing the work. But for those who stay disciplined, the reward is clear: a shot at quality companies without the distortion of banker-set pricing or institutional gatekeeping.

In the end, direct listings don't just test a company's fundamentals; they test yours as an investor. If you can tune out noise, analyze insider behavior, and track the flow of smart money, you can position yourself ahead of the crowd.

CASE STUDIES: DIRECT LISTINGS IN PRACTICE - SPOTIFY, SLACK, PALANTIR, AND COINBASE

Introduction

Direct listings have emerged as a notable alternative to traditional IPOs, allowing companies to go public without raising new capital or using underwriters. While not suitable for every business, direct listings appeal to companies seeking a more transparent, cost-effective route to the public markets. This case study explores four high-profile direct listings—Spotify, Slack, Palantir, and Coinbase—highlighting the motivations behind their decisions, strategic execution, and market outcomes.

Spotify: Pioneering Transparency in Public Listings

In 2018, Spotify became the first major company to pursue a direct listing on the New York Stock Exchange. Rather than issuing new shares, the company allowed existing shareholders to sell their stock directly to the public. The move was bold, bypassing traditional underwriters and eliminating the need for a capital raise. Spotify's motivation was twofold: to uphold its core value of radical transparency and to avoid the dilution and fees associated with a conventional IPO.

Several key factors enabled Spotify's successful debut:

- *Strong Brand Equity: With a global user base and industry leadership in streaming, Spotify did not require underwriter validation.*
- *Healthy Cash Reserves: The company was well-capitalized and had no immediate need for fundraising.*
- *Commitment to Transparency: Instead of a closed-door roadshow, Spotify hosted an open webcast for investors.*

Critics were skeptical, especially given the absence of a traditional price-setting mechanism and lock-up period. Yet, Spotify's shares traded with remarkable stability, setting a new precedent for how strong, well-known companies could access public markets on their own terms.

Slack: Market-Driven Pricing Meets Investor Confidence

In 2019, Slack followed Spotify's lead, executing a direct listing on the NYSE. The messaging platform eschewed the traditional IPO roadshow, enabling the market—not investment bankers—to determine its opening price. Slack's strategy mirrored Spotify's: leverage brand awareness, avoid dilution, and maintain control over the narrative.

Slack's listing highlighted several advantages of the direct listing approach:

- *Cost Savings: Slack avoided hefty underwriting fees, freeing capital for growth.*
- *Transparency: Investors were provided equal access to information, reinforcing trust in the company's model.*
- *Brand Strength: Slack's prominence within enterprise communication gave it wide visibility and investor appeal.*

Slack's shares opened well above the reference price, signaling market enthusiasm. However, like many tech companies, Slack faced volatility in the months following, underscoring that even innovative IPO models are not immune to post-listing challenges.

Palantir: A Hybrid Listing Strategy for Stability

Palantir's 2020 direct listing introduced an unconventional twist. To manage volatility and investor sentiment, the company implemented a modified lock-up provision—restricting insider sales to 20 percent of shares for 180 days. This hybrid model was designed to balance the liquidity benefits of a direct listing with some of the investor protections common in traditional IPOs.

Palantir's motivations were unique:

- *Navigating Market Skepticism: The company faced public scrutiny due to its government contracts and opaque operations.*
- *Mitigating Volatility: The staggered share release helped avoid the dramatic price swings sometimes seen in direct listings.*

While the lock-up was atypical for direct listings, Palantir demonstrated adaptability in aligning its listing mechanics with market expectations. The result was a measured debut, followed by significant trading volume and heightened public visibility.

Coinbase: Testing Market Appetite amid Crypto Volatility

Coinbase's direct listing in 2021 marked a milestone for the cryptocurrency sector and public market innovation. As the first major crypto exchange to go public, Coinbase leveraged a direct listing to avoid traditional underwriting and capitalize on the fervent interest in digital assets.

Coinbase's strategy revealed several key dynamics:

- *Sector Legitimacy: Going public through a direct listing signaled growing mainstream acceptance of crypto.*
- *Market Volatility: Coinbase's stock soared early, mirroring Bitcoin's rally, but later experienced sharp declines as crypto markets cooled.*
- *Transparency and Access: The listing provided institutional and retail investors with direct exposure to the company's performance.*

Despite the volatility, Coinbase's listing underscored how disruptive companies can leverage alternative routes to market while building investor confidence in emerging sectors.

DIRECT LISTINGS AS A STRATEGIC TOOL

While not suitable for all companies, direct listings have proven to be effective for brands with strong recognition, solid balance sheets, and a desire for greater transparency. Spotify and Slack succeeded by empowering the market to determine their value. Palantir adapted the model to balance investor expectations with internal risk management. Coinbase leveraged the listing to bring crypto into the financial mainstream.

These examples highlight that, when thoughtfully executed, direct listings can serve as powerful tools to access the public markets, especially for companies that prioritize flexibility, cost-efficiency, and shareholder equality.

REGULATION A+: DEMOCRATIZED IPOS WITH A TWIST

Regulation A+ offerings are often described as the "people's IPO," a gateway for startups and growth-stage companies to tap public capital without the red tape and cost of a traditional IPO. Enabled by the JOBS Act, Reg A+ has two tiers: Tier 1 allows offerings up to $20 million annually, while Tier 2 permits up to $75 million with stricter reporting requirements. But democratization doesn't mean de-risking.

While Reg A+ opens the door for broader participation, it also removes many of the safeguards that experienced investors rely on. Most Reg A+ issuers lack deep institutional support, third-party due diligence, or the rigor of GAAP-level financial auditing. For the retail investor, this means the potential for a ground-floor opportunity but also for a trapdoor under your feet.

STRUCTURAL RISKS IN REG A+ OFFERINGS

- Thin Floats: Many Reg A+ stocks enter the public markets with a float of less than 5 percent. With limited liquidity and few natural buyers beyond the initial crowd, prices can whipsaw dramatically. This structural illiquidity amplifies volatility and makes exits unpredictable, especially outside of news cycles.
- Marketing-Driven Demand: In the absence of a roadshow or institutional bookbuild, many Reg A+ issuers lean heavily on social media, influencers, or their existing customer base to promote the offering. These campaigns can spark massive short-term demand, but hype can easily outpace

substance. When sentiment cools, prices tend to fall fast and hard.

From an investor standpoint, this is not a space to rely on brand familiarity or emotional connection. It's a space to do rigorous homework. While Reg A+ can surface early-stage disruptors, many issuers are unprofitable, lightly regulated, and sometimes led by teams with limited public company experience.

HOW TO NAVIGATE REG A+ AS AN INVESTOR

- Study the Offering Circular (Form 1-A): These documents are the equivalent of a mini-prospectus. Look for details on burn rate, revenue concentration, and capital allocation. Weak disclosures or vague use of proceeds are red flags.
- Assess Float Control: Who controls the available shares post-IPO? If insiders retain most of the equity and retail owns the rest, there may be no institutional ballast to stabilize trading.
- Investigate Auditor Credibility: Many Reg A+ issuers work with lesser-known or unranked auditing firms. If the auditor has no track record with public companies, be cautious.
- Evaluate Customer-to-Investor Conversion: Companies that mobilize their user base to become shareholders (as Newsmax did) can create powerful early momentum, but that doesn't guarantee fundamentals. Check the revenue model. Check the losses. Check the roadmap.
- Watch for Future Dilution: Reg A+ companies often raise follow-on capital quickly, which can dilute

early shareholders. Study whether there's an equity line in place, a shelf registration ready to go, or language suggesting another raise is imminent.

At its best, Reg A+ empowers investors to get in early. At its worst, it enables issuers to capitalize on attention without accountability. The structure doesn't dictate the outcome, the quality of the business and the discipline of the investor do.

For those willing to dig beyond the surface, Reg A+ can offer asymmetric upside, particularly with mission-driven brands, strong communities, or underserved niches. But like any frontier, it favors the prepared. Know what you own, why you own it, and what can go wrong. In Reg A+, the line between movement and mania is thin, and only fundamental analysis can tell the difference.

CASE STUDY: NEWSMAX MEDIA'S DIRECT-TO-INVESTOR IPO

In 2025, Newsmax Media took an unconventional route to go public by conducting a direct-to-investor IPO. This approach bypassed traditional institutional underwriting and leveraged its loyal audience base to drive interest in its stock. While the initial market reaction was explosive, the long-term outcome highlighted key risks associated with sentiment-driven public offerings.

IPO Highlights

Newsmax's direct-to-investor IPO was characterized by:

- *Audience-Centric Strategy: The company capitalized on its established audience base to generate retail investor enthusiasm.*

- *Initial Surge: On its first day of trading, Newsmax›s stock price skyrocketed by 700 percent, fueled by concentrated retail demand and brand loyalty. While this dramatic surge highlights retail enthusiasm, it also underscores the risks of sentiment-driven valuations and low float dynamics, which can lead to sharp corrections when fundamentals don't align with hype.*
- *Subsequent Retreat: The stock quickly lost momentum due to structural challenges, including:*
    - *Low Float: Limited shares available for trading contributed to volatility.*
    - *Minimal Analyst Coverage: A lack of professional analysis left investors with little guidance on valuation.*
    - *Limited Institutional Support: The absence of institutional backing undermined long-term stability.*

Investor Takeaway

Newsmax Media's IPO offers valuable insights for both companies and investors:

Democratized Access Doesn't Guarantee Stability
While direct-to-investor models can broaden access, they may lack the stabilizing influence of institutional participation and professional underwriting.

Sentiment-Driven Valuations Often Revert Rapidly
Retail enthusiasm can drive significant short-term price increases, but such valuations are prone to sharp corrections when fundamentals do not support the hype.

Brand Loyalty Is Powerful but Insufficient Without Strong Fundamentals
Newsmax's loyal audience base generated initial interest, but the lack of robust financial metrics and institutional confidence ultimately led to price volatility and retreat.

Newsmax Media's direct-to-investor IPO demonstrated the potential of leveraging brand loyalty to attract retail investors but also underscored the risks of sentiment-driven offerings. Companies considering similar approaches must balance democratized access with strategies to ensure stability, while investors should remain cautious about chasing hype without evaluating underlying fundamentals.

WHY SPECIAL SITUATIONS MATTER

SPACs, direct listings, and Reg A+ offerings sit at the edges of the public market playbook, not because they're inferior but because they're different. These "special situations" operate outside the well-lit corridors of traditional underwriting. And that's precisely why they matter.

For the discerning investor, this perimeter is where the edge is born.

Each of these structures introduces informational asymmetry, moments when the market doesn't yet fully understand what it's looking at. In the early days of a SPAC merger, the first week of a direct listing, or the chaotic debut of a Reg A+ stock, price and value are often out of sync. That misalignment creates risk but also opportunity.

WHAT MAKES SPECIAL SITUATIONS SPECIAL?

- Under-Researched Deals: Traditional IPOs arrive on the market with analyst coverage, institutional backing, and roadshow narratives. Special situations often debut in silence. For investors who do their own work, this silence is a signal, not a drawback.

- Pricing Inefficiencies: Without underwriters controlling the narrative, or with retail sentiment distorting the order book, pricing in these deals can swing wildly. That creates entry points that don't exist in more "efficient" transactions.
- Narrative-Driven Valuations: Many special situations hinge on compelling but polarizing stories. A SPAC may promise a future rooted in unproven tech. A Reg A+ company may ride the momentum of a loyal fanbase. A direct listing may forgo promotion altogether. These extremes create gaps between perception and reality, gaps that investors can exploit if they understand the business better than the crowd.

From a portfolio construction standpoint, these deals serve a very specific purpose: they are not for broad exposure; they are for strategic bets. When approached correctly, special situations can deliver convex returns, outsized gains relative to the risk, especially if you catch a misunderstood business before it enters mainstream awareness.

But here's the key: these aren't "buy and forget" investments. They're active positions that require monitoring, reassessment, and a constant reevaluation of the narrative. You're not just buying a company; you're buying time, attention, and the possibility that the market will eventually catch up to your thesis.

In a world where most public equities are priced to near-perfection, special situations remind us that alpha still exists for those willing to do the work.

BUILDING YOUR INVESTMENT FRAMEWORK

Special situations demand a different lens, one that balances agility with rigor. These aren't plug-and-play trades. Each opportunity must be approached with a customized playbook that accounts for stage, structure, and story. The goal isn't just to find potential winners; it's to manage risk, allocate conviction appropriately, and exit before the market shifts under your feet.

1. Know the Stage

Your strategy should match where the deal is in its life cycle:

- Pre-Deal SPAC: Before a target is announced, this is effectively a bet on the sponsor. Look for seasoned operators with a history of value creation, not first-timers chasing a trend. Evaluate their industry focus, deal criteria, and past exits. Pre-deal SPACs can offer downside protection via redemption rights, but only if you're disciplined.
- SPAC Merger Announcement: This is where volatility spikes, and so does the opportunity. Dissect the target's financials. Ask if the projections are credible or just narrative-driven. Compare valuation multiples to public peers. Is the PIPE strong? Who's anchoring it? The first forty-eight hours post-announcement are when sentiment outruns substance; your edge is in staying rational.
- Direct Listing Launch: Early trades are raw price discovery. Watch the volume and order book. Track insider Form 4 filings for early confidence (or the lack of it). Let the volatility settle. You're not trying to buy the pop; you're looking for the floor.

- Reg A+ Offering: Here, the due diligence burden shifts squarely onto you. Read the Form 1-A like it's a forensic exercise. Is the revenue model sustainable? Who are the auditors? Is the company being propped up by fan loyalty or real economics? Thin floats and retail enthusiasm can lift prices fast, but they fall even faster when sentiment fades.

2. Conduct Due Diligence

Treat each of these vehicles like a venture investment, not a public equity. That means asking hard questions:

- Is there real product traction or just a compelling story?
- Has the team built and scaled a business before?
- Are projections grounded in reality or built on aggressive assumptions and TAM dreams?
- Is the valuation justified relative to comps, stage, and sector dynamics?

The earlier you invest in the life cycle, the more your outcome depends on qualitative factors, founder skill, product-market fit, and capital discipline. As the company matures, financials take on greater weight. Adjust your lens accordingly.

3. Plan Your Exit

Every entry must have a planned exit. These are not "set and forget" assets.

- Lockups: Know when insiders can sell. These expiration windows often precede sharp drops in price due to sudden surges in liquidity.

- Liquidity Constraints: Especially in Reg A+ deals, floats are thin and spreads are wide. Can you exit your position without moving the market?
- Insider Selling: Watch for clusters of executive sales post-listing. Sometimes it's normal. Sometimes it's a signal they don't believe in the long-term story.

Your investment framework should be dynamic, not static. It should evolve with the structure of the deal and the behavior of the company. Above all, it should keep you grounded when narratives take flight and crowds rush in.

In special situations, discipline isn't optional; it's your competitive edge.

THE FUTURE OF SPECIAL SITUATIONS

The market's infatuation with special situations in 2020-2021 gave way to a needed recalibration. What emerged from the shakeout is a quieter, more selective evolution, one that favors substance over spectacle.

- SPACs have matured. The post-hype era ushered in "SPAC 4.0", where sponsor compensation is increasingly tied to long-term performance and merger structures include investor-friendly protections like earnouts, milestone triggers, and longer lockups. The low-quality deals are fading. What's left is a refined subset of SPACs focused on complex sectors like space tech, biotech, or advanced manufacturing, areas where traditional IPOs often hesitate.
- Direct listings are evolving. Companies like Roblox and Squarespace have explored hybrid models that combine the transparency of direct listings with the

capital-raising utility of IPOs. As exchanges adapt and regulatory clarity improves, we're likely to see more tailored listings, especially from companies that value market-driven pricing and brand control over banker-led pricing narratives.

- Reg A+ is gaining traction, but under the microscope. More consumer-facing brands are using Reg A+ to convert loyal audiences into early investors. But as investor experiences vary widely, so does scrutiny. A few high-profile failures could invite tighter regulatory oversight. On the flip side, successful campaigns could accelerate the trend of "community capital," especially for mission-driven companies and cultural brands.

In short: the experimentation phase is over. The refinement era has begun.

PRACTICAL TIPS FOR ENGAGING WITH SPECIAL SITUATIONS

1. Start Modestly
   Special situations are high-variance by nature. Begin with small positions and increase exposure only when conviction is backed by data, not headlines.
2. Follow Leadership Relentlessly
   In SPACs and Reg A+, the deal is only as strong as the people behind it. Scrutinize sponsors and founders: Have they operated public companies before? Are they communicative post-listing? Do they execute?

3. Use Warrants as Strategic Tools
   SPAC warrants can offer leveraged exposure with defined risk, but timing is everything. Understand redemption windows, warrant terms, and dilution potential before deploying.
4. Monitor Float and Liquidity
   Thin floats create price dislocations, on both the upside and downside. Always ask: Can I enter and exit efficiently? Who else is in this trade?

INTEGRATING SPECIAL SITUATIONS INTO YOUR PORTFOLIO

- Know Your Risk Tolerance
  Special situations are not for the faint of heart. Expect volatility. If a -30 percent drawdown rattles you, even temporarily, position size accordingly.

- Diversify with Intent
  Don't overload on unproven narratives. Balance exposure across different structures (SPAC, Reg A+, direct listing) and sectors (tech, consumer, industrial) to spread idiosyncratic risk.

- Align Time Horizon to Thesis
  Some of these plays, especially in frontier sectors, require patience. Don't pair long-term narratives with short-term expectations.

- Stay Engaged
  These are not "buy and hold" positions. Monitor filings, earnings calls, insider activity, and macro factors. Your edge comes from staying a half-step ahead of the crowd.

CHAPTER 10

FINAL TAKEAWAYS

SPACs, direct listings, and Reg A+ are not fringe finance; they're frontline innovations in capital formation. Each offers a chance to engage with businesses and ideas that might otherwise remain private or inaccessible. But they demand more from investors: more research, more skepticism, and more agility.

These structures reveal inefficiencies that legacy IPOs often obscure. That's the opportunity. But they also reveal risk faster and punish complacency harder.

If you can navigate these channels with discipline, curiosity, and strategic precision, special situations become more than a footnote in your portfolio. They become the edge, the asymmetric opportunities that most investors miss because they're looking in the wrong places or asking the wrong questions.

In a world of efficient markets and crowded trades, this is where the gems are buried. Just don't forget to bring a shovel.

CHAPTER 11

The Global IPO Landscape - Risks and Opportunities for Investors

For many international companies, listing on a U.S. exchange represents an opportunity to access the world's largest capital market, gain global visibility, and potentially secure higher valuations with greater liquidity. While the U.S. market does offer deep capital access, valuation uplift compared to domestic exchanges depends on factors like sector performance and investor sentiment. Emerging economies may not always experience higher valuations due to geopolitical risks and regulatory hurdles. However, the presence of a diverse and sophisticated investor base, including institutional investors, hedge funds, and retail traders, can result in enhanced price discovery and greater long-term capital inflow.

Additionally, U.S. exchanges are known for robust corporate governance and investor protection frameworks, which can enhance confidence and attract more capital. Unlike some emerging markets where regulatory transparency is inconsistent, companies that successfully meet SEC disclosure requirements often gain higher investor trust. This increased transparency and stringent reporting standards allow investors to better assess risks, ultimately leading to a more efficient and liquid market for international IPOs.

Listing on NASDAQ or the NYSE also enhances credibility, providing prestige and global branding that can benefit partnerships, supplier relationships, and cross-border expansion. Companies that successfully list in the U.S. often find it easier to attract strategic investors and negotiate better terms in future fundraising rounds. Moreover, dual-listing opportunities with Hong Kong, London, or other financial centers allow companies to leverage multiple capital markets while maintaining the credibility and financial rigor associated with a U.S. exchange.

From an investor perspective, it is crucial to assess whether the true benefits of a U.S. listing justify the expected valuation premiums and whether a company's business fundamentals, governance structure, and long-term growth prospects support sustainable value creation. While access to U.S. capital markets is a strong advantage, investors should also analyze risks such as regulatory hurdles, geopolitical factors, and compliance challenges that could impact a foreign company's performance post-IPO.

ROADBLOCKS AND EVOLVING REGULATIONS FOR CHINESE FIRMS LISTING IN THE U.S.

In the early 2000s, there was a wave of Chinese IPOs in the U.S., many of which relied on the Variable Interest Entity (VIE) structure to circumvent foreign ownership restrictions on sensitive industries such as technology and media. This model allowed foreign investors to gain economic exposure to Chinese firms without direct equity ownership. However, the structure has legal ambiguities, as it relies on complex contractual agreements rather than actual shareholder rights, leading to potential enforcement risks if Chinese authorities ever choose to disallow the practice.

Regulatory scrutiny has significantly increased in recent years, driven by fraud scandals, accounting irregularities, and geopolitical tensions between the U.S. and China. Several high-profile Chinese companies, such as Luckin Coffee, faced delisting or significant penalties after financial misconduct was uncovered, prompting U.S. regulators to impose stricter disclosure and auditing requirements. The SEC has since introduced the Holding Foreign Companies Accountable Act (HFCAA), which mandates that foreign companies provide full access to their audit workpapers. Non-compliance with these requirements for three consecutive years may result in mandatory delisting from U.S. exchanges, a risk that investors must carefully monitor.

Additionally, China has implemented its own restrictions on foreign listings, requiring firms to obtain approval from the China Securities Regulatory Commission (CSRC) before pursuing an overseas IPO. This move is part of Beijing's broader effort to control data security and capital outflows, particularly for companies handling sensitive user information. For instance, the crackdown on Didi Global's U.S. IPO in 2021, which led to heavy regulatory penalties and voluntarily delisted from the NYSE in December 2022 under pressure from Chinese authorities rather than being forcibly delisted. This underscores the dual-layered risks of investing in Chinese firms that list abroad.

From an investor perspective, these evolving regulations present risks and opportunities. On one hand, increased regulatory oversight can lead to greater transparency and reduced fraud risk for well-managed Chinese firms. On the other hand, heightened scrutiny from U.S. and Chinese authorities increases uncertainty, as companies may face compliance hurdles, increased reporting burdens, or even abrupt policy shifts that impact their market value. Additionally, political tensions between the U.S. and China could lead to further restrictions, affecting investor confidence and liquidity in Chinese ADRs (American Depositary Receipts).

Investors considering Chinese IPOs must conduct thorough due diligence on regulatory filings, corporate governance practices, and financial disclosures. Companies that demonstrate compliance with U.S. and Chinese regulatory frameworks, maintain strong internal auditing controls, and operate in non-sensitive sectors may present better risk-adjusted opportunities. However, the potential for delisting, forced repatriation, or political intervention remains an inherent risk, requiring a well-calibrated investment strategy when considering exposure to Chinese equities in U.S. markets.

CASE STUDY: BRILLIANCE CHINA AUTOMOTIVE HOLDINGS LTD. – THE FIRST CHINESE IPO ON A U.S. EXCHANGE

In October 1992, Brilliance China Automotive Holdings Ltd. made history as the first Chinese company to list on a U.S. stock exchange. Trading under the ticker symbol NYSE:CBA, the company raised $80 million in its New York Stock Exchange debut, with shares priced at $16. The IPO was met with overwhelming demand and was oversubscribed nearly 12 times, reflecting strong global investor interest. This milestone marked the beginning of a new era in international capital markets and set a precedent for future Chinese listings abroad.

Strategic Significance

Brilliance China's listing on the NYSE came during a transformative period in China's economic reform. The IPO represented a strategic leap forward for Chinese enterprises seeking access to global capital and recognition in Western markets.

Access to Capital:
The $80 million raised through the IPO provided Brilliance with essential growth capital. These funds were critical to expanding operations and strengthening the company's competitive position in China's emerging automotive sector. The NYSE listing also enhanced the company's appeal to institutional investors and opened new funding channels beyond domestic borders.

Global Visibility:
Brilliance China's debut gave it international credibility and set the tone for how Chinese companies could compete for investor attention on the world stage. The listing positioned Brilliance not only as a domestic automotive player but as a pioneer among Chinese companies with cross-border ambitions.

Challenges and Adaptations
Listing on the NYSE required Brilliance to overcome several legal and regulatory hurdles. As the first Chinese issuer in the U.S. market, it had no playbook to follow.

Ownership Restrictions:
At the time of the IPO, Chinese regulations prohibited foreign ownership in key domestic companies. To navigate this, Brilliance established a holding company in Bermuda. Shares of this offshore entity were then listed and traded on the NYSE as American Depositary Shares (ADS). Meanwhile, a Chinese-registered investment fund held operational control through contractual agreements, ensuring the company remained compliant with local ownership laws while allowing foreign investors to participate indirectly.

Compliance with U.S. Regulations:
As a U.S.-listed entity, Brilliance was subject to the reporting standards and disclosure requirements of the Securities

and Exchange Commission. This included full compliance with U.S. Generally Accepted Accounting Principles (GAAP). Meeting these standards required Brilliance to significantly improve its financial transparency and adapt its corporate governance structure to align with Western expectations.

High Maintenance Costs:
While the benefits of listing were substantial, so were the costs. Annual fees for legal and accounting compliance were estimated at around $1 million. Over time, as trading volume in the company's shares declined, these fixed costs became increasingly difficult to justify. Ultimately, they contributed to Brilliance's decision to delist from the NYSE.

Post-IPO Performance
The initial excitement surrounding Brilliance's IPO gradually faded as operational headwinds mounted.

Operational Decline:
By the early 2000s, the company faced intensifying competition in China's now crowded automotive market. Brilliance struggled to keep pace with more innovative rivals. Weak product development, growing debt burdens, and legal disputes further eroded its performance.

Delisting from the NYSE:
In 2007, Brilliance voluntarily delisted from the NYSE, citing low trading volume and the high cost of maintaining its listing. However, the company continued to trade on the Hong Kong Stock Exchange.

Key Takeaways for Investors

Pioneering Role:
Brilliance China's IPO proved that Chinese companies could access U.S. capital markets using creative corporate structures. The listing demonstrated how offshore entities could

be used to comply with domestic ownership restrictions while still tapping foreign investment.

Regulatory Compliance:
The company's adherence to SEC regulations and GAAP accounting helped establish a precedent for financial transparency among Chinese issuers. However, the cost of compliance was significant, highlighting the importance of scale and trading volume to justify a U.S. listing.

Sustainability Challenges:
While Brilliance's IPO attracted strong demand, long-term success proved elusive. The company's inability to innovate and maintain operational excellence ultimately led to its withdrawal from the U.S. market. This reinforced the idea that access to capital must be matched with strategic execution and adaptability.

Conclusion

Brilliance China Automotive Holdings Ltd.'s IPO on the NYSE was a landmark event in the evolution of global equity markets. It opened the door for other Chinese companies to follow, illustrating the potential rewards of cross-border listings. At the same time, it exposed the risks involved in navigating two regulatory environments, sustaining high compliance costs, and meeting the long-term expectations of international investors. For future issuers and investors alike, Brilliance's story offers valuable lessons in ambition and caution.

DIFFERENCES IN FINANCIAL REPORTING STANDARDS AND TRANSPARENCY

International companies often face significant challenges in aligning their financial disclosures with U.S.

standards. Many foreign markets follow International Financial Reporting Standards (IFRS) or regional frameworks, which can differ substantially from U.S. Generally Accepted Accounting Principles (GAAP) in key areas such as revenue recognition, asset valuation, and expense classification. These discrepancies can create reporting inconsistencies that make it difficult for investors to accurately compare financial statements across companies listed on U.S. exchanges.

The transition to U.S. reporting can be especially challenging for companies from emerging markets, where accounting oversight and auditing practices may not meet the stringent transparency requirements of the SEC and Public Company Accounting Oversight Board (PCAOB). Many firms lack internal controls robust enough to ensure compliance with Sarbanes-Oxley Act (SOX) requirements, increasing the risk of financial misstatements. Over the years, several high-profile cases, such as Luckin Coffee's fabricated revenue scandal, have underscored the risks associated with companies that fail to meet proper accounting standards. As a result, the SEC has intensified its scrutiny of foreign issuers, particularly those from jurisdictions with limited audit access.

Regulatory bodies in the U.S. have taken a proactive approach to financial transparency. Under the Holding Foreign Companies Accountable Act (HFCAA), foreign companies must allow PCAOB auditors to inspect their financial workpapers. Companies that fail to comply for three consecutive years face potential delisting, a critical risk for investors. While some firms, particularly in China, have negotiated agreements to avoid delisting, uncertainty remains around the enforceability of such agreements and their long-term sustainability.

Corporate governance expectations also vary widely across markets, creating further challenges for international firms listing in the U.S. Many foreign companies operate with highly centralized ownership structures, where founders or government-linked entities retain significant control. These structures can lead to weaker board independence, limited shareholder rights, and governance policies that favor insiders over minority investors. In contrast, U.S. markets emphasize stronger disclosure standards, independent boards, and shareholder protections, which may not align with a company's existing corporate culture.

For investors, conducting thorough due diligence on a company's financial reporting and governance structure is essential before making investment decisions. This includes analyzing auditor history, past regulatory findings, board composition, and executive compensation policies to identify potential red flags. Companies that demonstrate clear transparency, adherence to SEC and PCAOB requirements, and robust corporate governance frameworks will be better positioned to gain investor confidence and sustain long-term value in the U.S. market. However, those that fail to meet these evolving standards face increased risk of regulatory action, reputational damage, and diminished investor trust.

COMPLIANCE CHALLENGES FOR FOREIGN FIRMS IN THE U.S.

Once a company lists on a U.S. exchange, maintaining compliance with SEC regulations, exchange requirements, and investor expectations becomes an ongoing challenge. Unlike domestic issuers, foreign companies register their IPOs under Form F-1 rather than the standard S-1 filing, which comes with different reporting requirements.

One key distinction is that foreign issuers are allowed to file financial reports semi-annually instead of quarterly, which can limit the availability of up-to-date financial data for investors. While this flexibility may reduce administrative burdens for foreign firms, it also means that investors have fewer opportunities to evaluate company performance, increasing the risk of unexpected financial downturns or governance issues going unnoticed for longer periods.

Compliance costs for maintaining a U.S. listing can be substantial, particularly for smaller foreign companies that may not have the necessary internal financial and legal infrastructure to meet stringent SEC requirements. Ongoing costs include audit fees, legal expenses, investor relations efforts, and adherence to U.S. accounting standards. These expenses can strain companies that are not adequately capitalized, leading some to voluntarily delist from U.S. exchanges or seek alternative listing venues with fewer regulatory hurdles. In recent years, an increasing number of international firms, particularly from China, have opted to transition their listings to Hong Kong or their home exchanges rather than sustain the cost and scrutiny of a U.S. listing.

For companies that do not voluntarily delist, the risk of involuntary delisting remains a significant concern. The Holding Foreign Companies Accountable Act (HFCAA) stipulates that firms failing to comply with U.S. audit requirements for three consecutive years will be forcibly removed from U.S. exchanges, posing a direct risk to investors holding shares in non-compliant issuers. Beyond regulatory non-compliance, companies that fail to meet minimum stock price and market capitalization thresholds—such as NASDAQ's requirement to maintain a $1.00 minimum bid price for thirty consecutive trading days—may also face delisting procedures. Such companies may attempt to execute reverse stock splits or secure additional capital to avoid this outcome, but in many cases, sustained poor performance leads to delisting and migration to over-the-counter (OTC) markets, where liquidity and investor protections are significantly reduced.

From an investor's perspective, evaluating a foreign company's ability to sustain long-term compliance with U.S. regulations is critical before committing capital. Due diligence should include reviewing historical financial disclosures, auditor reports, SEC comment letters, and the company's ability to meet governance standards. Investors should also assess how well management communicates regulatory risks and engages with shareholders to address compliance concerns. Companies with strong governance structures, proactive regulatory engagement, and a track record of timely reporting are far more likely to maintain exchange listing status and deliver sustainable value. Meanwhile, companies that struggle with compliance, face repeated SEC inquiries, or rely on regulatory exemptions should be approached with heightened caution.

RISKS AND OPPORTUNITIES IN FOREIGN IPOS ON U.S. EXCHANGES

Foreign IPOs on U.S. exchanges present unique investment opportunities and heightened risks. For investors, these companies offer exposure to high-growth sectors, untapped markets, and international diversification, often providing access to industries and consumer bases not readily available in the U.S. Many emerging-market companies operate in fast-growing industries such as fintech, e-commerce, biotechnology, and renewable energy, where the potential for long-term expansion can be significant. As a result, investors looking for portfolio diversification and early-stage growth opportunities may find foreign IPOs an attractive option.

However, these opportunities come with inherent risks that investors must carefully evaluate. One major factor is currency risk, as fluctuations in exchange rates can directly impact the financial performance of foreign companies and influence investor returns. A depreciation of the company's home currency against the U.S. dollar can erode profits, while currency controls or restrictions on repatriation of funds can limit investor flexibility. Political and regulatory uncertainties also play a critical role, as government policies, trade restrictions, and geopolitical conflicts can create volatility in foreign stocks. Tensions between the U.S. and China, for instance, have led to restrictions on Chinese companies accessing U.S. capital markets, further complicating the investment landscape. Investors should be mindful of cross-border trade policies, taxation differences, and compliance with evolving international regulatory frameworks when assessing foreign IPOs.

Additionally, foreign companies often face higher volatility and price swings, particularly in the micro-cap space, where investor sentiment and liquidity constraints can amplify fluctuations. The SEC has taken steps to manage this volatility by enhancing disclosure requirements and strengthening oversight of foreign issuers. However, foreign IPOs frequently attract speculative trading activity, leading to unpredictable post-listing performance. Many newly listed foreign companies experience significant price surges upon debut, followed by sharp declines once initial hype fades, making timing and due diligence essential for investors.

Another key concern is corporate governance standards, which vary widely across international markets. Investors should carefully evaluate a foreign company's board structure, shareholder protections, and adherence to U.S. governance norms. Some jurisdictions have less stringent investor protections, increasing the risk of insider control, opaque financial reporting, and limited shareholder influence. Dual-class share structures, common in some foreign firms, may also reduce investor voting rights and create challenges in holding management accountable.

For investors considering foreign IPOs, conducting comprehensive due diligence is crucial. Reviewing regulatory filings, financial statements, auditor reports, and management backgrounds can help identify potential red flags. Additionally, understanding the company's competitive positioning, revenue sources, and long-term growth strategy is essential to distinguishing sustainable investment opportunities from short-term market fads. Companies that demonstrate regulatory compliance, financial transparency, and strong governance frameworks are more likely to succeed in U.S. markets, while those with uncertain compliance, aggressive accounting practices, or excessive reliance on government subsidies should be approached with caution.

While foreign IPOs provide exciting opportunities for investors seeking international exposure, they require a disciplined investment approach. Understanding geopolitical risks, currency movements, governance challenges, and market volatility will be key in navigating the potential rewards and pitfalls of these investments. As the regulatory landscape continues to evolve, staying informed and adopting a risk-adjusted strategy will help investors maximize their exposure to global growth while mitigating downside risks.

CASE STUDY: ALIBABA GROUP HOLDING LTD. (2014 IPO)

Alibaba Group's Initial Public Offering (IPO) on the New York Stock Exchange in September 2014 was a historic moment in capital markets. Raising $25 billion, it became the largest IPO in history and symbolized China's rising influence in global tech. Alibaba's decision to list in the

United States was strategic. It provided the company with greater global visibility, deep liquidity, and access to a broader investor base. Yet, behind the headlines, Alibaba's IPO also spotlighted the complex regulatory and geopolitical terrain faced by international issuers.

Strategic Use of Variable Interest Entity (VIE) Structure

Alibaba's IPO relied on a Variable Interest Entity (VIE) structure to navigate China's foreign ownership restrictions in sensitive industries such as e-commerce and technology.

Mechanism:
The VIE model involved the establishment of offshore holding companies in jurisdictions like the Cayman Islands. These entities entered into contractual arrangements that allowed them to control Alibaba's onshore Chinese operations without formal equity ownership.

Legal Ambiguity:
This structure, though effective, exists in a regulatory gray zone. Chinese law does not explicitly endorse or prohibit VIEs, leaving them vulnerable to policy reversals. If Chinese regulators were to disallow such arrangements, foreign investors could lose economic exposure to Alibaba's core assets.

Investor Risk:

Alibaba disclosed these risks in its SEC filings, cautioning that regulatory changes in China could threaten the validity of the VIE structure. For investors, the message was clear: access to Alibaba's growth would come with legal uncertainty.

Benefits of U.S. Listing
Alibaba's decision to list on the New York Stock Exchange was calculated to deliver long-term strategic advantages.

Enhanced Corporate Governance:
Compliance with U.S. regulatory requirements, including oversight from the Securities and Exchange Commission, imposed higher standards of transparency and accountability. For investors, this provided greater confidence in Alibaba's governance framework compared to a domestic Chinese listing.

Global Visibility and Prestige:
The NYSE listing elevated Alibaba's global profile. It signaled to markets that the company was prepared to compete with Western tech giants like Amazon. The prestige of a U.S. listing also helped attract significant institutional capital, increasing both liquidity and valuation.

Access to Capital:
The IPO opened the door to one of the world's deepest capital pools. Proceeds were used to fund acquisitions and international expansion, providing the fuel Alibaba needed to maintain its competitive edge.

Challenges Post-IPO:
Despite the IPO's initial success, Alibaba faced a series of post-listing challenges that tested the resilience of its business model and investor confidence.

Regulatory Scrutiny:
The introduction of the Holding Foreign Companies Accountable Act (HFCAA) required foreign issuers to provide full access to audit workpapers. Noncompliance could lead to delisting from U.S. exchanges. For Alibaba, the cost of ongoing compliance was substantial. Adhering to Sarbanes-Oxley regulations and maintaining audit transparency required significant operational resources.

Geopolitical Risk:
Ongoing tensions between the United States and China created a volatile backdrop. Disputes over data privacy, national security, and trade policy placed additional pressure on Chinese companies with U.S. listings. Concurrently, Alibaba also faced increased domestic scrutiny from Chinese regulators, including criticism over counterfeit products on its Taobao platform.

Corporate Governance Concerns:
Critics highlighted Alibaba's concentrated ownership structure and its reliance on the VIE model as key weaknesses. These factors limited shareholder rights and raised concerns about investor protection. While the company met U.S. disclosure standards, its internal control remained heavily centralized.

Key Takeaways for Investors

- *Strategic Use of VIEs: Alibaba's VIE structure enabled it to access global capital markets despite Chinese ownership restrictions. However, investors needed to weigh the legal uncertainty attached to this workaround.*
- *Benefits of U.S. Listing: The company gained access to better governance, improved visibility, and ample capital through its NYSE listing. These advantages reinforced the appeal of cross-border IPOs for emerging-market companies.*
- *Regulatory Challenges: The case of Alibaba emphasized how dual scrutiny both domestic and foreign regulators can complicate a company's post-IPO trajectory.*

Conclusion

Alibaba's 2014 IPO remains a landmark case in international finance. It illustrates how global companies can unlock massive growth by tapping into U.S. capital markets and how legal and regulatory complexities can shadow even the most successful listings. For investors, the offering showcased the upside of global diversification and the critical need for due diligence in understanding structures like VIEs. While the rewards were substantial, the risks were equally clear.

TRENDS IN INTERNATIONAL LISTINGS

As global markets shift, new trends are emerging in international IPOs, reshaping how companies access capital and how investors participate in cross-border opportunities. Companies are increasingly pursuing dual and secondary listings across major financial hubs such as Hong Kong, London, and New York as part of a broader strategy to diversify investor bases, enhance liquidity, and reduce geopolitical exposure. The shift is particularly noticeable in Chinese firms, many of which are seeking alternative listing venues outside the U.S. due to regulatory tensions and delisting risks tied to stricter audit requirements and evolving trade policies. At the same time, U.S.-listed firms are exploring dual listings in Europe and Asia to tap into regional investor demand and increase market stability.

The rise of tech-enabled IPO access has also fundamentally changed the landscape, making it easier for issuers and investors to participate in global listings. Digital trading platforms and fintech innovations, such as blockchain-based securities and AI-driven investment tools, are democratizing IPO participation, allowing retail investors to engage with international offerings more efficiently. The expansion of online brokerage services and fractional share ownership models has made foreign IPOs more accessible to individual investors who previously lacked exposure to non-U.S. markets. Additionally, Special Purpose Acquisition Companies (SPACs) have gained traction as an alternative route for international firms to go public, bypassing the traditional IPO process and accelerating access to U.S. capital markets.

Regulatory frameworks continue to evolve in response to increased cross-border listings, with governments adjusting their policy approaches to foreign companies. The U.K. and Singapore have introduced reforms to attract more IPOs, offering competitive listing requirements and tax incentives, while China has implemented tighter controls on overseas listings, particularly for companies handling sensitive data or strategic industries. The SEC and PCAOB (Public Company Accounting Oversight Board) remain focused on enhancing disclosure and audit transparency for foreign issuers, which has led to heightened scrutiny of international IPOs in the U.S. These regulatory shifts present both risks and opportunities for investors, as companies adapt their listing strategies to navigate geopolitical pressures, investor sentiment, and compliance requirements.

FINAL TAKEAWAYS

For investors, understanding these trends is critical to identifying opportunities and mitigating risks in international IPOs. Companies pursuing secondary listings often have mature business models and strong financial track records, making them less volatile than first-time IPOs in emerging markets. However, the macroeconomic and political landscape remains a key factor, as shifting trade policies, currency fluctuations, and regional economic stability can impact foreign stocks in unpredictable ways. Additionally, investors must assess governance structures, reporting transparency, and long-term commitment to U.S. market standards when evaluating cross-listed companies.

The global IPO landscape is evolving rapidly, driven by technological advancements, regulatory shifts, and changing capital flows. As companies seek to hedge against market instability and geopolitical risks, dual and cross-border listings are likely to grow. For investors, staying informed about international regulatory developments, digital trading innovations, and geopolitical dynamics will be essential to navigating this new wave of global public market access.

CHAPTER 12

The Future of IPO Investing

The future of IPO investing is being shaped by a convergence of innovation, democratization, and regulatory transformation. As capital markets continue to evolve, new technologies and participation models are redefining the traditional boundaries of who can invest, how companies go public, and what success looks like in the public arena.

For the first time in modern finance, a retail investor in Cape Town can participate in a New York-based IPO from their phone, while a fintech startup in Jakarta prepares to list simultaneously in Hong Kong and on the Nasdaq. Meanwhile, an AI algorithm in London is assessing risk factors in real-time, and a regulatory shift in Singapore is paving the way for tokenized securities to become commonplace. This isn't fiction. It's the unfolding story of public market access, and investors need to know how to read the next chapter.

This chapter looks forward, exploring the key forces that will shape IPO investing in the decade ahead, including artificial intelligence (AI), blockchain, SPACs, retail investor access, and global regulatory trends. The opportunities are immense, but so are the challenges. For investors, understanding these shifts is essential for thriving in a dynamic and increasingly digital investment landscape.

AI AND THE TRANSFORMATION OF IPO INTELLIGENCE

Artificial Intelligence is fundamentally reshaping the mechanics of IPO investing. From predictive analytics in IPO pricing models to real-time sentiment analysis and algorithmic allocation strategies, AI enhances efficiency and insight throughout the process. Investment banks and institutional investors increasingly leverage AI to evaluate S-1 filings, monitor demand signals during roadshows, and optimize IPO bookbuilding.

In particular, natural language processing (NLP) models are being used to parse and score IPO prospectuses, identifying red flags in risk disclosures, leadership bios, or inconsistent revenue narratives. These tools allow underwriters to flag anomalies early and help institutional investors adjust pricing models with greater precision. For example, some firms now use AI to simulate multiple demand curves based on investor profiles, dynamically adjusting allocations during bookbuilding to optimize post-listing performance.

Retail investors are also benefiting. AI-powered platforms now offer predictive tools that assess IPO quality based on historical trends, peer comparisons, and market sentiment. For example, automated scoring systems can flag high-risk IPOs or highlight undervalued entries based on a mix of structured and unstructured data. Platforms like EquityZen, Zignaly, and Atom Finance are increasingly incorporating AI-driven insights into their IPO dashboards, allowing retail participants to evaluate deals with a level of sophistication previously limited to hedge funds and research desks.

In a 2024 study published by the CFA Institute, many institutional respondents reported using AI tools in IPO analysis, with sentiment analysis and risk modeling cited as the most common applications. Yet, despite the advantages, these tools are not without risk. AI systems can amplify existing market biases, misinterpret context, or prioritize short-term momentum signals over long-term fundamentals. "Model overfitting" remains a common challenge, especially when models are trained on limited historical IPO datasets, which tend to be skewed by bull-market cycles.

This raises important questions about explainability and accountability. Black-box algorithms, while efficient, can obscure how and why certain IPOs are flagged as attractive or risky. Regulators have begun to take notice.

For investors, AI is a double-edged sword. It can surface opportunities faster and more accurately, but it must be used as a complement, not a crutch. Effective IPO investing still requires human judgment, critical thinking, and a disciplined understanding of fundamentals, governance, and market context. The most successful investors will use AI not as a decision-maker but as a decision enhancer, filtering noise, flagging anomalies, and sharpening focus on what truly matters.

CASE STUDY: RENAISSANCE CAPITAL – AUGMENTING HUMAN INSIGHT WITH AI

As one of the leading independent research firms focused exclusively on IPOs, Renaissance Capital has long been recognized for its analytical depth and data-driven strategies. In recent years, the firm has integrated artificial intelligence into its research workflows, enhancing speed and precision in IPO screening and valuation.

Renaissance's proprietary IPO Intelligence platform leverages machine learning to analyze historical pricing dynamics, sector-specific momentum, and investor sentiment signals across more than 1,500 IPOs. Natural language processing (NLP) algorithms are deployed to scan S-1 filings and distill key financial metrics, use-of-proceeds summaries, and competitive risk disclosures into standardized comparison frameworks. This allows analysts to benchmark each new IPO against a curated database of prior deals across sector, market cap, and performance profile.

However, Renaissance does not use AI to replace human judgment. Instead, AI functions as a second lens, helping analysts filter noise, identify anomalies, and challenge assumptions in early-stage analysis. The firm's IPO ETF (ticker: IPO) reflects this hybrid approach, combining quant factors with curated analyst discretion to select high-conviction positions.

The result: a faster, more responsive research engine that preserves rigor while adapting to the velocity of modern markets. For investors, Renaissance's model offers a glimpse into how AI can be thoughtfully integrated, not to disrupt human insight but to sharpen it.

THE RISE AND REGULATION OF SPACS

Special Purpose Acquisition Companies (SPACs) surged during the 2020–2021 cycle, raising over $160 billion across hundreds of deals and temporarily eclipsing traditional IPOs as the preferred path to public markets for early-stage and growth companies. This boom was driven by favorable market liquidity, pandemic-era risk appetite, and the promise of a faster, less burdensome path to capital. While the initial euphoria has since subsided, SPACs remain an enduring and evolving fixture in the public markets, particularly within capital-intensive or innovation-driven sectors such as clean energy, space technology, biotech, and autonomous mobility.

Unlike traditional IPOs, which involve extensive SEC filings, roadshows, and underwriter-led bookbuilding, SPACs offer a more streamlined process. A SPAC is essentially a publicly traded shell company formed for the sole purpose of acquiring a private business, bringing it public through a merger rather than an offering. This model allows target companies greater control over valuation, deal timing, and forward-looking projections, elements often constrained in traditional IPOs.

From an investor standpoint, SPACs can offer early access to companies at the frontier of innovation, often before they meet the revenue or profitability thresholds expected in IPOs. But these deals carry structural and behavioral risks that cannot be overlooked. The incentives for SPAC sponsors, who typically receive a 20 percent stake in the post-merger entity, often regardless of long-term performance, can lead to misaligned interests. In many cases, deals were rushed to meet de-SPAC timelines, resulting in poor target quality or inadequate due diligence.

Performance data underscores these concerns. According to a 2023 report by Goldman Sachs, more than 70 percent of post-merger SPACs underperformed the Russell 3000 within twelve months of listing, and many fell below their $10 offering price shortly after completing a merger. This volatility, compounded by earnings misses, accounting restatements, or executive turnover, triggered a wave of investor lawsuits and heightened regulatory scrutiny.

The SEC has since responded with proposed reforms aimed at restoring accountability and transparency. Key initiatives include:

- Requiring SPAC sponsors to disclose conflicts of interest and financial incentives more clearly.

- Holding underwriters liable for due diligence failures in de-SPAC mergers, effectively aligning them with traditional IPO standards.
- Limiting the use of overly optimistic forward-looking projections, particularly in sectors with limited visibility into revenue streams or regulatory approval.

If enacted, these rules would close critical loopholes and bring SPAC disclosures closer in line with the rigor expected in standard IPOs. For investors, this means fewer surprises and a better framework for comparing SPAC targets to traditionally listed peers.

SPACs are no longer a shortcut; they are a parallel track that demands equal levels of scrutiny. As the market matures, sophisticated investors will increasingly apply traditional IPO due diligence filters to SPAC targets: analyzing capital structure, path to profitability, insider alignment, and post-merger integration plans. The firms that treat SPACs with the same analytical rigor as IPOs will be best positioned to separate viable long-term growth stories from speculative hype.

CASE STUDY: LORDSTOWN MOTORS – WHEN HYPE OUTPACES FUNDAMENTALS

Lordstown Motors, an electric vehicle startup, merged with DiamondPeak Holdings Corp., a SPAC, in October 2020 at the height of EV market enthusiasm. The deal valued Lordstown at $1.6 billion and was backed by aggressive, forward-looking projections of commercial truck production.

However, within months, red flags emerged. The company faced allegations of inflated preorders, missed production milestones, and executive departures. A short-seller report from Hindenburg Research claimed Lordstown had "no viable product," triggering SEC investigations. By mid-2021, the stock had fallen over 80 percent from its post-merger highs.

Lordstown's collapse highlighted multiple SPAC-related pitfalls: optimistic projections unchecked by underwriters, misaligned incentives, and inadequate due diligence. The company eventually filed for bankruptcy in 2023, becoming a cautionary tale of the speculative frenzy that defined the first SPAC wave.

CASE STUDY: DRAFTKINGS - A SPAC THAT STUCK THE LANDING

In contrast, DraftKings—a digital sports betting platform—merged with Diamond Eagle Acquisition Corp. in April 2020. Unlike many SPAC targets, DraftKings had strong brand equity, an established customer base, and a clear path to revenue growth, particularly as U.S. states moved to legalize online sports wagering.

Post-merger, DraftKings maintained strong market momentum, quickly becoming a leader in the online gaming space. The company used its public capital to expand into new markets, invest in technology, and drive user acquisition. While the stock has faced volatility, DraftKings remains a high-profile example of a SPAC-backed company with sustainable fundamentals and long-term investor alignment.

DraftKings' success underscores the importance of deal quality, sector tailwinds, and disciplined execution. It also illustrates that SPACs, when used strategically, can still serve as a viable path to market leadership.

THE BLOCKCHAIN REVOLUTION AND IPOS

Blockchain technology is poised to fundamentally alter how securities are issued, settled, and recorded, introducing a level of efficiency, transparency, and accessibility that challenges the very infrastructure of today's capital markets. The concept of tokenized IPOs, in which shares are issued and traded directly on a blockchain ledger, promises real-time settlement, fractional ownership, automated compliance, and reduced dependency on centralized intermediaries such as transfer agents and clearinghouses.

The benefits are compelling. Smart contracts can streamline regulatory compliance, ensuring automatic enforcement of rules around share transfer restrictions, voting rights, and dividend distributions. Transactions, recorded immutably on distributed ledgers, create a transparent audit trail that can reduce fraud, error, and back-office reconciliation costs. For issuers, the use of blockchain can dramatically compress the IPO timeline and open access to a broader, more global investor base.

One early example is INX Limited, a Gibraltar-registered company that launched the first SEC-registered tokenized IPO in 2020. The offering, built on Ethereum, raised over $80 million and provided investors with digital tokens representing equity-like claims. While relatively modest in scale, INX demonstrated that compliant blockchain-based capital raising is technically feasible and legally viable. Since then, companies in Europe, Asia, and the Middle East have explored similar digital securities offerings, often backed by government-led innovation sandboxes or specialized licenses.

Jurisdictions leading the charge include Switzerland, which has integrated digital asset laws into its financial framework through the Swiss DLT Act, and Singapore, where the Monetary Authority of Singapore (MAS) supports tokenized equity through its Project Guardian initiative. In Germany, Deutsche Börse has launched its own digital exchange platform, while Hong Kong and the UAE are developing regulatory pathways for security token offerings (STOs).

By contrast, U.S. regulators have taken a more cautious approach. The SEC has yet to issue clear, dedicated guidelines for tokenized IPOs, preferring to regulate on a case-by-case basis. Concerns around custody, investor protection, market manipulation, and AML/KYC compliance continue to delay broader adoption.

The 2023 collapse of crypto-related firms like FTX has only sharpened regulatory scrutiny, underscoring the need for robust controls before mainstream adoption can occur. That said, the agency has acknowledged blockchain's potential in improving market infrastructure, and pilot programs (such as those under the SEC's FinHub) continue to explore future pathways.

For investors, this landscape presents opportunities and challenges. Early adopters of blockchain-enabled IPOs may benefit from:

- Access to previously illiquid or private markets via fractionalized ownership,
- Lower transaction costs,
- Real-time portfolio rebalancing and settlement, and
- Participation in a global 24/7 trading ecosystem.

However, they must also navigate:

- Technological risks (e.g., smart contract vulnerabilities, platform interoperability),
- Custodial uncertainties (how and where tokenized securities are held),

- Jurisdictional inconsistencies in how digital securities are taxed, regulated, or enforced, and
- Counterparty risk, particularly in the case of decentralized exchanges (DEXs) lacking formal accountability structures.

Furthermore, the current lack of standardized reporting and benchmarking for

RETAIL INVESTOR ACCESS: A PERMANENT SHIFT

The democratization of IPOs is no longer theoretical. It has become a defining feature of the modern capital market. Fintech platforms such as Robinhood, SoFi, and Webull have dismantled long-standing barriers to entry, enabling individual investors to access IPO shares once reserved for institutional players and ultra-high-net-worth clients. This tectonic shift has created a new class of IPO participants: younger, mobile-first, and deeply engaged through digital channels.

Retail participation in IPOs surged during the 2020–2021 cycle, with retail investors accounting for as much as 20–25 percent of IPO allocations in select deals, according to Nasdaq. Robinhood's own IPO in 2021, which allocated up to 35 percent of its shares to retail users via its IPO Access feature, exemplified this rebalancing of market access. These investors are not just passive participants; they are active contributors to price discovery, post-listing liquidity, and momentum shifts during the crucial first days of trading.

Yet, this inclusivity comes with real challenges. Retail investors, often influenced by social media platforms like Reddit, TikTok, or X (formerly Twitter), are more susceptible to emotion-driven decision-making. Fear of missing out (FOMO), herd behavior, and speculative exuberance can distort IPO pricing efficiency and amplify volatility. High-profile cases such as Rivian and Instacart show how investor sentiment, fueled by hype cycles, can dramatically impact first-day price swings, regardless of underlying fundamentals.

The learning curve is steep. Many retail investors underestimate the complexity of IPO structures, such as lock-up expirations, greenshoe provisions, or insider ownership dilution. Without clear educational resources and disclosure tools, these investors are at risk of entering IPOs with unrealistic expectations or inadequate risk frameworks.

To address this, platforms must evolve beyond access providers to become educational stewards. SoFi, for instance, now offers pre-IPO briefings, real-time market commentary, and post-listing performance tracking to guide its users. Robinhood has introduced alerts tied to IPO quiet periods, and Webull has launched deeper analytics to help users assess deal quality. These enhancements mark the beginning of a more informed retail cohort, but they are not yet industry standard.

From an institutional investor perspective, retail capital is no longer peripheral; it is now a variable to model and monitor. Understanding retail demand patterns, sentiment drivers, and digital distribution channels has become essential to forecasting IPO pricing outcomes and aftermarket performance. As more issuers seek to include a retail allocation in their roadshow strategy, underwriters must refine how they segment demand and shape investor communication.

The participation of retail investors introduces dispersion and democratization. On one hand, it widens the shareholder base and injects liquidity into early trading. On the other hand, it introduces behavioral volatility that must be carefully managed through pricing discipline, education, and transparency.

In the years ahead, we can expect to see hybrid IPO structures that integrate institutional rigor with retail inclusion, combining algorithmic allocations, digital onboarding, and post-IPO engagement strategies. For investors who understand this new terrain, retail flows are not just noise; they are signals, rich with data about sentiment, conviction, and sector momentum.

CONTROLLING THE FLIP – HOW PLATFORMS ARE MANAGING RETAIL SPECULATION

With increased retail participation in IPOs has come a rise in short-term trading behavior, particularly IPO flipping, where shares are sold within hours or days of the public debut to lock in quick gains. While this tactic can drive liquidity, it also introduces volatility and undermines issuer efforts to build a stable shareholder base.

To combat this, platforms like SoFi and Robinhood have implemented cooling-off policies designed to discourage speculative churn:

- *SoFi's IPO "30-Day Rule": Investors who sell IPO shares allocated through SoFi within thirty days of the listing date may be restricted from participating in future IPOs. This policy aims to foster long-term ownership and align investor behavior with issuer goals.*
- *Robinhood's Lockout Enforcement: Robinhood flags users who flip IPO shares and may suspend their IPO access privileges for a defined period. The platform also issues pre-trade reminders that outline the impact of early selling on account eligibility.*

These measures reflect a broader industry shift; platforms are beginning to curate IPO participation based on engagement, education, and holding behavior, not just account size or activity. For retail investors, this means playing the long game isn't just wise; it's increasingly required.

GLOBALIZATION AND REGULATORY CONVERGENCE

The IPO landscape is no longer defined by a single market or listing pathway. In today's interconnected financial ecosystem, companies are increasingly evaluating multi-jurisdictional listings, cross-border SPAC combinations, and dual listings on global exchanges such as the Nasdaq, Hong Kong Stock Exchange (HKEX), Euronext, and London Stock Exchange (LSE). This globalization reflects a desire to tap into regional investor bases, hedge against geopolitical volatility, and benefit from jurisdictional strengths, be it deeper liquidity in the U.S., favorable regulation in Europe, or strong domestic alignment in Asia.

In recent years, high-profile companies such as Alibaba, NIO, and BioNTech have adopted dual-listing strategies to broaden their capital base and reduce reliance on any single market. Meanwhile, rising interest in cross-border SPAC mergers, such as Grab's $40 billion deal via Altimeter Growth Corp, illustrates how alternative listing mechanisms are being deployed to reach public markets faster, especially in emerging and innovation-heavy economies.

However, with global access comes global complexity.

Each exchange operates under distinct listing rules, disclosure requirements, investor protections, and audit frameworks. Companies must navigate a patchwork of regulatory regimes, often with conflicting standards around key issues like data privacy, financial transparency, shareholder rights, and executive accountability. For example, a company listing simultaneously in the U.S. and China must reconcile Sarbanes-Oxley audit rules with China's data localization laws, a challenge that has led to rising tensions and even forced delisting.

At the heart of this fragmentation lies the absence of a harmonized global disclosure regime. While efforts are underway, driven by organizations such as the International Organization of Securities Commissions (IOSCO) and the Financial Stability Board (FSB), progress is uneven.

Nowhere is this divergence more visible than in the ongoing standoff between the U.S. and China. The Holding Foreign Companies Accountable Act (HFCAA) requires foreign issuers to allow U.S. regulators access to audit workpapers or face delisting, putting pressure on Chinese firms listed on U.S. exchanges. In response, Chinese regulators have imposed outbound listing approval frameworks, citing national security concerns around data exposure. This dual layer of scrutiny introduces significant uncertainty for investors holding American Depositary Receipts (ADRs) or participating in cross-border IPOs.

For investors, this environment demands more than sector knowledge or financial modelling; it requires regulatory fluency. The ability to understand:

- Jurisdictional differences in reporting standards and audit regimes,
- Political and regulatory risks related to the listing venue,
- Legal structures like Variable Interest Entities (VIEs), often used by Chinese tech firms to bypass ownership restrictions, and
- the implications of currency controls, capital repatriation limits, or tax treaties . . .

. . . will become essential for assessing the long-term viability and governance quality of foreign IPOs.

STRATEGIC TAKEAWAY:

The future of global IPOs lies not just in broader access but in smarter participation. Investors who develop a deep understanding of listing frameworks, geopolitical risk, and disclosure asymmetries will have a distinct edge. In an age of market nationalism and cross-border capital realignment, *where* a company lists is as strategic as how it performs.

FINAL TAKEAWAYS

IPO investing is entering a transformative chapter, one defined by digital access, AI-driven intelligence, global capital flows, and a rapidly shifting regulatory landscape. The traditional gatekeepers of the public markets have been joined by new platforms, new structures, and new participants, all of which are redrawing the boundaries of how companies go public and who gets to participate.

Yet, amid this evolution, the core principles of successful IPO investing remain unchanged: disciplined valuation, rigorous due diligence, a clear understanding of governance, and a commitment to long-term value creation. What's changing is the toolkit and the terrain.

Investors must now navigate offerings structured via SPACs, tokenized shares issued on blockchain networks, retail-driven IPO momentum cycles, and cross-border listings entangled in geopolitical complexity. This requires not just technical fluency but strategic foresight: the ability to synthesize financial analysis, regulatory interpretation, and technological signals into a coherent investment thesis.

But this evolution isn't only technological; it's personal. The next generation of IPO investors is not just watching CNBC; they're reading S-1s on Reddit, trading on their phones during lunch breaks, and building thesis-driven portfolios from their living rooms. They are curious, resourceful, and globally aware. They are also vulnerable to noise, hype, and rapid-fire market shifts. For them—and for all investors—winning in this new market demands more than access. It requires intention.

The winners in this new era will be those who adapt fastest and think deepest. They will leverage machine learning without losing sight of fundamentals. They will assess risk in terms of both financial metrics and jurisdictional nuance, and they will understand that while hype may drive headlines, conviction is built through context.

The future of IPOs is not just about capital formation; it is about capital evolution: a more connected, inclusive, transparent marketplace where information moves faster, access is broader, and expectations are higher. For investors willing to blend wisdom with curiosity, data with discernment, and speed with structure, the opportunity ahead is nothing short of extraordinary.

This is not just a new phase for IPOs. It's a new playbook. And it belongs to those prepared to write it.

CONCLUSION

FROM UNDERSTANDING TO ACTION: THE NEXT ERA OF IPO INVESTING

As you turn the final pages of this book, you're not simply closing a cover. You're stepping into a marketplace full of possibility, challenge, and potential reward. The world of Initial Public Offerings is no longer confined to the privileged few. It is expanding, evolving, and increasingly accessible to informed, disciplined investors who are ready to participate with intention.

Throughout *The Investor's IPO*, we've explored the full spectrum of IPO investing. From historical foundations to modern innovations, from decoding the prospectus to evaluating global listings, and from identifying red flags to recognizing what makes a winner, this book has equipped you with a framework to approach IPOs with confidence, clarity, and critical thinking.

But knowledge alone is not enough. The most successful IPO investors are those who combine insight with execution. They resist hype, ask hard questions, and commit to long-term thinking rather than chasing short-term gains. They understand that IPOs are not lottery tickets. They are strategic inflection points where risk and opportunity intersect and where preparation makes all the difference.

The IPO landscape will continue to shift. New technologies will emerge, regulations will adapt, and investor behavior will evolve. Your advantage lies not in predicting the next trend but in being prepared to assess it when it arrives. With the tools and strategies outlined in this book, you now have a repeatable process to evaluate any IPO, regardless of market conditions.

This is not the end of your journey. It is the beginning of a more empowered and strategic approach to investing in public markets.

So, take the next step. Whether it is your first IPO or your fiftieth, approach it with the discipline of a professional and the curiosity of a lifelong learner.

Because in this new era of investing, it is not just about who gets in; it is about how they play once they do.

ENDNOTES

Chapter 1: Modern IPO Essentials - Understanding Today's Market and the Origins of IPO Investing

- Neal, L. (2005). The Dutch and English East India Companies: Diplomacy, Trade and Violence in the Early Modern World. Cambridge University Press. [Dutch East India Company IPO, 1602]
- Dale, R. (2016). The First Crash: Lessons from the South Sea Bubble. Princeton University Press. [South Sea Bubble, 1720]
- U.S. Congress. (2012). Jumpstart Our Business Startups (JOBS) Act, Pub.L. 112–106.
- U.S. Congress. (1933, 1934). Securities Act of 1933 and Securities Exchange Act of 1934.
- Securities and Exchange Commission. (n.d.). SEC Regulatory Guidance.
- Securities and Exchange Commission. (2004). Google Inc. Form S-1 Registration Statement. [Google IPO, Dutch auction]

Chapter 2: Evolution in the Digital Era - Examining the Impact of Technology on the IPO Process

- Coinbase Global, Inc. (2021). Form S-1 Registration Statement. [Coinbase direct listing]
- Robinhood Markets, Inc. (2021). Form S-1 Registration Statement. [Robinhood IPO and IPO Access]
- Beyond Meat, Inc. (2019). Form S-1 Registration Statement. [Beyond Meat IPO]
- U.S. Congress. (2012). Jumpstart Our Business Startups (JOBS) Act.
- FINRA. (n.d.). Rules and Guidance on Digital IPOs and Crowdfunding.
- Company websites: SoFi Invest, Robinhood, Webull. [Online IPO access platforms]

Chapter 3: The Importance of IPOs in the Economy

- Kauffman Foundation. (2021). The Economic Impact of High-Growth Startups: IPOs and Job Creation.
- Stanford University. (2019). Patent Activity and Innovation Post-IPO.
- Arm Holdings plc. (2023). Form F-1 Registration Statement. [Arm Holdings IPO]
- Moderna, Inc. (2018). Form S-1 Registration Statement. [Moderna IPO]
- Morgan Stanley. (2024). AI IPO Pipeline and Market Outlook.

- Sapphire Ventures. (2024). AI Startups and ARR Benchmarks.
- EY. (2024). AI Investment and ROI Survey.
- McKinsey Global Institute. (2018). Notes from the AI Frontier: Modeling the Impact of AI on the World Economy.
- C3.ai, Inc. (2020). Form S-1 Registration Statement. [C3.ai IPO]
- BIO (Biotechnology Innovation Organization). (2023). Biotech IPOs and FDA Drug Approvals.
- Airbnb, Inc. (2020). Form S-1 Registration Statement. [Airbnb IPO]
- Saudi Arabian Oil Company (Saudi Aramco). (2019). IPO Prospectus. [Saudi Aramco IPO]

Chapter 4: IPO Investment Stages - Key Steps and Strategies

- Crunchbase. (2023). Stripe Company Profile & Funding. [Stripe pre-IPO valuation]
- TechCrunch. (2023, March 15). Stripe raises $6.5B at $50B valuation.
- Maplebear Inc. (Instacart). (2023). Form S-1 Registration Statement. [Instacart IPO]
- Robinhood Markets, Inc. (2021). Form S-1 Registration Statement. [Robinhood IPO]
- Nasdaq, Inc. (2024). IPO Statistics and Market Performance.

- New York Stock Exchange (NYSE). (2024). IPO Listings Data.

Chapter 5: Evaluating IPO Prospects - Identifying Winners and Avoiding Pitfalls

- Uber Technologies, Inc. (2019). Form S-1 Registration Statement. [Uber IPO]
- Rivian Automotive, Inc. (2021). Form S-1 Registration Statement. [Rivian IPO]
- Ritter, J. (University of Florida). (n.d.). IPO Underperformance Studies.
- Industry reports: S&P Global, Bloomberg, Reuters. [Financial metrics and sector benchmarks]

Chapter 6: Understanding the IPO Prospectus - Decoding the Investment Narrative

- Ritter, J. (University of Florida). (n.d.). IPO Underperformance Studies.
- U.S. Securities and Exchange Commission. (n.d.). SEC Filings and Regulatory Guidance.
- Company S-1/F-1 filings as cited in previous chapters.

Chapter 7: IPO Success vs. Failure - Key Characteristics

- Ritter, J. R. (University of Florida). (n.d.). IPO Underpricing and Long-Run Performance Studies.

- Loughran, T., & Ritter, J. R. (2004). Why Has IPO Underpricing Changed Over Time? Financial Management, 33(3), 5–37.
- Uber Technologies, Inc. (2019). Form S-1 Registration Statement. U.S. Securities and Exchange Commission.
- Beyond Meat, Inc. (2019). Form S-1 Registration Statement. U.S. Securities and Exchange Commission.
- Rivian Automotive, Inc. (2021). Form S-1 Registration Statement. U.S. Securities and Exchange Commission.

Chapter 8: Gaining IPO Access and Market Information

- Robinhood Markets, Inc. (2021). Form S-1 Registration Statement. U.S. Securities and Exchange Commission.
- SoFi Technologies, Inc. (2021). Company Website and Press Releases on IPO Access.
- Webull Financial LLC. (n.d.). Company Website and IPO Access Information.
- FINRA. (n.d.). Rules and Guidance on Retail IPO Access.
- U.S. Securities and Exchange Commission. (n.d.). Investor Education on IPOs.

Chapter 9: Trading Strategies

- Ritter, J. R. (University of Florida). (n.d.). IPO Performance and Aftermarket Trading Studies.
- Nasdaq, Inc. (2024). Market Data and IPO Trading Performance.
- New York Stock Exchange (NYSE). (2024). IPO Trading Statistics.
- S&P Global Market Intelligence. (2024). Trading Volatility and Lock-Up Expiration Data.
- Bloomberg. (2024). IPO Aftermarket Performance Reports.

Chapter 10: Special Situations – SPACs, Direct Listings, and Alternative IPO Structures

- U.S. Securities and Exchange Commission. (n.d.). SPACs, Direct Listings, and Alternative IPO Guidance.
- Spotify Technology S.A. (2018). Form F-1 Registration Statement. U.S. Securities and Exchange Commission.
- Slack Technologies, Inc. (2019). Form S-1 Registration Statement. U.S. Securities and Exchange Commission.
- Coinbase Global, Inc. (2021). Form S-1 Registration Statement. U.S. Securities and Exchange Commission.
- Renaissance Capital. (2024). SPAC IPO Market Reports and Data.

- FINRA. (n.d.). SPAC and Alternative Listing Rules and Investor Alerts.

Chapter 11: Foreign Companies Listing in the U.S. - Opportunities and Risks

- Arm Holdings plc. (2023). Form F-1 Registration Statement. U.S. Securities and Exchange Commission.
- Alibaba Group Holding Limited. (2014). Form F-1 Registration Statement. U.S. Securities and Exchange Commission.
- NIO Inc. (2018). Form F-1 Registration Statement. U.S. Securities and Exchange Commission.
- U.S. Securities and Exchange Commission. (n.d.). Guidance on Foreign Private Issuers and ADRs.
- PwC. (2023). Cross-Border IPO Trends and Regulatory Insights.

Chapter 12: The Future of IPO Investing - Trends and Sustainability

- Morgan Stanley. (2024). AI IPO Pipeline and Market Outlook.
- McKinsey Global Institute. (2018). Notes from the AI Frontier: Modeling the Impact of AI on the World Economy.
- EY. (2024). IPO Trends and ESG Integration Survey.
- BIO (Biotechnology Innovation Organization). (2023). Biotech IPOs and Innovation Reports.

- Bloomberg. (2024). Sustainable Finance and ESG IPO Data.
- U.S. Securities and Exchange Commission. (n.d.). ESG Disclosure Guidance and Future Trends in Public Markets.

www.ingramcontent.com/pod-product-compliance
Lightning Source LLC
LaVergne TN
LVHW022208200926
848481LV00006B/1889
* 9 7 9 8 9 8 9 1 7 1 1 3 2 *